RECIPES FROM THE ORKNEY ISLANDS

RECIPES FROM THE ORKNEY ISLANDS

RECIPES

FROM THE ORKNEY ISLANDS

Edited by
EILEEN WOLFE

GORDON WRIGHT PUBLISHING
55 MARCHMONT ROAD, EDINBURGH EH9 1HT
SCOTLAND

SBN 903065 21 5

Cover Illustration by Gordon Wright

Line illustrations by Marianne Birkeland
Photographs on pages 37, 38, 67, 68, by Gunnie Moberg

Printed in Scotland by Lindsay & Co. Ltd.
Bound in Scotland by Letts Andersons Ltd.

INTRODUCTION

We have collected these recipes from the fascinating Orkney Islands to let you savour the very best in Orkney cookery.

To produce the book, we circulated all the Orkney branches of the Scottish Women's Rural Institutes, hotels and restaurants throughout the islands, and everyone else whom we felt could make an interesting contribution.

We also encouraged people to devise original recipes, using local produce such as meat, seafood, cheese, grain, sweetmeats, whisky etc. and give it an Orkney name. The response was excellent.

In making the final selection, we tried to give priority to what we considered to be original recipes with a distinctive Orkney flavour, and we hope you will test and taste what we consider to be an exciting new collection to take into your kitchen.

Special thanks are due to:

Mr Gerry Meyer of *The Orcadian* who kindly printed details of our quest and brought in many contributions.

Mr Howie Firth of B.B.C. Orkney who broadcast on his morning programme and stimulated much interest.

Mr Tam MacPhail of Stromness Books and Prints and Mr John Leonard of Kirkwall who kindly distributed leaflets to their bookshop customers.

All this effort contributed to the final production and we are indeed indebted to everyone concerned.

CONTENTS

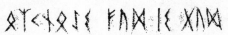

CONTENTS

SOUP

ORCADIAN OATMEAL SOUP

1 large onion	1 oz oatmeal
2 small carrots	1 pint stock
1 leek	¾ pint milk
A little turnip or cabbage	Seasoning
Fat	

METHOD

1. Prepare and dice all the vegetables.
2. Toss the vegetables in the melted fat until coated.
3. Add the oatmeal and fry for a few minutes.
4. Add the stock and the seasoning and simmer for 45 minutes.
5. The soup can now be sieved or liquidised if required.
6. Add the milk and re-heat before serving.

H. Firth, Kirkwall

SCOTCH BROTH

1-1½ lb mutton, chopped	3 tablespoons pearl barley
2 medium carrots	1 cup dried peas
2 medium onions	6 pints of water
½ medium turnip	Salt and pepper

METHOD

1. Soak the barley and peas overnight in cold water.
2. Put the peas, barley, meat and water into a pan with a pinch of salt.
3. Cover pan and bring slowly to the boil.
4. Skim carefully.
5. Peel and dice the vegetables and add to the pan.
6. Simmer for 1½-2 hours, then season to taste.

J. Wilkie, Evie

HOLM VEGETABLE SOUP

1 small carrot	2 pints water
1 small turnip	½ pint milk
1 small onion	1 oz flour
½ a leek	1 oz butter
1 stick celery	½ small bay leaf
Salt and Pepper	

METHOD

1. Shred the vegetables.
2. Melt the butter and toss the vegetables in it.
3. Add the bay leaf and water and boil until the vegetables are tender.
4. Mix the flour and milk together and add to the pan. Boil for a few minutes to cook the flour, stirring continuously.
5. Take out bay leaf, season well and serve hot.

D. Laughton, Holm

RED POTAGE

½ lb haricot beans	4 small tomatoes
1 oz butter	1 stick celery
1 large onion	3 pints water, or stock
1 beetroot	

METHOD

1. Peel onion, beetroot and tomatoes. Roughly chop all the vegetables.
2. Melt butter and add all ingredients. Cook gently for a few minutes.
3. Add water or stock.
4. Season and simmer for two hours.
5. Sieve, reheat and serve piping hot.

Mrs Findlay, Stromness

CABBAGE SOUP

1 large cabbage   2 large potatoes,
2 oz butter   thinly sliced
2 pints milk   Seasoning

METHOD

1. Wash the cabbage well and let it stand in salted water for one hour.
2. Rinse the cabbage and shred it finely.
3. Melt the butter in a stewpan, put in the cabbage and stir until the cabbage has absorbed all the butter.
4. Add enough water to cover and stew till tender.
5. Add the potatoes, and when they are cooked, mash them up to thicken the soup.
6. Season, add the milk and boil up to serve.

P. Johnston, Stromness

SPRING SOUP

2 pints stock   1 tablespoon each:
½ teaspoon castor   shredded lettuce,
   sugar   carrot and turnip
1 tablespoon rice   (diced)
Seasoning

METHOD

1. Boil the stock, add the rice, carrots and turnip and cook for 15 minutes.
2. Add the lettuce, sugar and seasoning and simmer till tender.

L. Grieve, Kirkwall

TOMATO SOUP

2 lb tomatoes
1 large onion
½ oz butter
2 pints stock
Seasoning

2 oz lean cooked ham,
   chopped
1 tablespoon sago
½ teaspoon sugar

METHOD

1. Slice the tomatoes and onions and fry them with the ham in the butter for 20 minutes, then rub through a fine sieve.
2. To this purée, add the stock, sago, sugar and salt and pepper to taste.
3. Bring to the boil and simmer until the sago is clear.

I. Hourston, Kirkwall

CAULIFLOWER SOUP

4 pints clear stock
Small cauliflower
Chopped parsley

Parmesan cheese
Cayenne pepper

METHOD

1. Pour boiling water over the cauliflower then plunge it into cold water.
2. Cut the cauliflower into small pieces, and boil in salted water until tender. Strain and put the cauliflower into the soup tureen.
3. Bring the stock to the boil and pour it over the cauliflower.
4. Sprinkle with cayenne pepper and finely chopped parsley and serve with grated Parmesan cheese.

E. Harvey, Stromness

12

CHICKEN BROTH

1 boiling chicken
2 oz rice
1 carrot
1 leek
Parsley

1 onion
4 pints water
Seasoning
1 blade of mace

METHOD

1. Simmer the chicken in the water for 1½ hours.
2. Remove the chicken from the water and add salt.
3. Chop the vegetables and add them to the stock with the rice and the blade of mace. Boil for a further 30 minutes. Skim when necessary.
4. Season to taste and serve with a sprinkling of chopped parsley.

T. Moar, Birsay

CARROT SOUP

5 carrots
2 onions
2 sticks celery
Turnip

1 teaspoon sugar
Knob of butter
Stock
Seasoning

METHOD

1. In 3 pints of well-seasoned stock boil the chopped vegetables.
2. Pulp the boiled vegetables through a sieve, add the butter and sugar.
3. Boil for 15 minutes to serve piping hot.

K. Wilson, Stromness

13

POTATO SOUP

1 lb potatoes
1 large onion
1 oz butter
1 oz flour
Pepper and salt

3 pints weak stock
2 tablespoons cream
1 dessertspoon finely
   chopped parsley

METHOD

1. Slice the onion finely and put it into a saucepan with the butter. Fry without browning for 15 minutes, stirring constantly.
2. Add the stock, and the potatoes cut into slices. Stir until soup boils, skim, and continue boiling until the potatoes are tender.
3. Rub all through a sieve, season, and put back into the saucepan to re-boil.
4. Mix the flour with the cream and stir into the soup.
5. Add the finely chopped parsley and serve.

E. Harvey, Stromness

WINTER VEGETABLE SOUP

Turnip
Carrot
Potato
Onion

Celery
Sweet herbs
Butter
Seasoning

METHOD

1. Melt a large knob of butter in a pan and toss equal quantities of chopped vegetables until they are brown.
2. Add water, seasoning and herbs and boil until tender.
3. Serve with toasted bread.

L. Young, Stromness

SCOTS KALE

1 cup barley	Kale
½ lb fresh beef	Salt
2 leeks	Water

METHOD

1. Put the barley in cold water and bring to the boil. Remove any scum.
2. Chop the beef finely and add to the soup pot with a little salt. Boil for 3 hours.
3. Chop the kale and leeks and add to the soup. Continue boiling until the greens are tender.
4. Season to taste.

N. Wylie, Kirkwall

SCOTTISH HERRING SOUP

2 small onions, finely chopped	14 oz can tomatoes
4 herrings, cleaned and boned	1 pint water
1 oz butter	3 tablespoons malt vinegar
2 oz mushrooms	Salt and pepper

METHOD

1. Cut the herrings into ½-inch pieces and add with other ingredients to water.
2. Bring to the boil and simmer gently for about 30 minutes until onions are ready.

H. Garson, Sandwick

15

BEETROOT SOUP

2 beetroots
3 onions
2 pints stock

3 tablespoons vinegar
1 tablespoon brown sugar
Seasoning

METHOD

1. Boil the beetroots until tender and rub off the skins.
2. Chop the beetroot and onions finely and add to the stock.
3. Stir in the vinegar and sugar and bring to the boil.
4. Season to taste.

K. Wilson, Stromness

BRUSSELS SPROUTS SOUP

1 lb Brussels sprouts
3 oz butter
1 oz flour
2 pints white stock
Salt

½ pint milk
White pepper
½ teaspoon castor
sugar

METHOD

1. Trim the discoloured leaves off the sprouts, wash them well, and let them stand in a basin of cold salted water for about an hour, then drain them.
2. Boil a saucepan of water and add a dessertspoon of salt for each quart of water and boil the sprouts for 15-20 minutes. Drain well and squeeze out as much moisture as possible.
3. Put the sprouts into a mortar and pound them until quite smooth then rub them through a sieve.
4. Put this purée into a clean saucepan, gradually stir in

16

the stock and season to taste with white pepper, salt and half a teaspoon of castor sugar. Bring to the boil.

5. Rub the butter into the flour and stir this into the soup.
6. Boil the milk in a separate saucepan, and just before serving the soup add the boiling milk to it.
7. Serve with small croûtons of toasted bread.

I. Hourston, Kirkwall

FISH SOUP

2 lb white fish
½ pint shrimps
2 oz butter
1 pint milk
2 oz flour
3 pints water
2 carrots
Pepper and salt

1 leek
½ stick of celery
Bunch of herbs (bayleaf,
    thyme and parsley)
Blade of mace
1 teaspoon chopped
    parsley

METHOD

1. Chop the fish into pieces and put them into a saucepan with three pints of cold water.
2. Add the vegetables thinly sliced, the herbs and the mace. Bring to the boil and skim.
3. Add the seasoning and boil for two hours until the vegetables are quite tender.
4. Strain as much of the soup as possible through a sieve.
5. Melt the butter in a saucepan. Mix in the flour, then gradually stir in the milk. Stir constantly until it boils.
6. Return the soup to its saucepan, and add the thickened milk, stirring until it almost boils.
7. Just before serving, add the finely chopped parsley and the shrimps.

L. Flett, Orphir

B

LOBSTER SHELL SOUP

½ lb lobster shell   1 carrot
2 oz butter   1 turnip
1 whiting (cooked)   1 onion
2 oz flour   Celery
2 pints stock   Herbs and seasoning
Mace

METHOD

1. Clean the lobster shell and pound with the butter until quite fine.
2. Put lobster shell and butter into a pan and heat to dissolve, then fry for a few minutes, adding flour.
3. Add stock, herbs, vegetables and whiting.
4. Boil for half an hour.
5. Add more stock if it is too thick.
6. Strain and re-heat, adding a little cream.
7. Serve very hot.

D. Laughton, Holm

OXTAIL SOUP

1 lb oxtail   1 dessertspoon vinegar
2 onions   1 wineglass port wine
2 carrots   1 teaspoon black pepper
Turnip   Sweet herbs

METHOD

1. Steep the oxtail in cold water for 2 hours.
2. Put the oxtail into water with the vegetables, sweet herbs and a teaspoon of black pepper.
3. Cover closely, and when it boils, skim off the fat.
4. Simmer for 3 hours.
5. Add the vinegar and port wine to serve.

P. Tulloch, Kirkwall

BEEF BROSE

Beef stock   Oatmeal

METHOD

1. After beef has been boiled and removed from the pot,
   skim off the fat with part of the liquor and boil it in a
   saucepan.
2. Toast a bowl of oatmeal before the fire until it is nicely
   browned.
3. Stir the liquor into the oatmeal until it is a good soup
   consistency.
4. Serve immediately.

N. Kirk, Kirkwall

LENTIL SOUP

½ lb brown lentils   2 oz streaky bacon
   (soaked for 3 hours)   Bouquet garni
2 onions, chopped   2½ pints stock
2 carrots, chopped   Seasoning

METHOD

1. Dice the bacon and heat in a saucepan until the fat
   begins to run then add the onion and cook for 2-3
   minutes.
2. Add the drained lentils, seasoning, carrot and stock,
   bring to the boil and put in the bouquet garni.
3. Simmer for 1-1½ hours until the lentils are soft.

E. Leslie, Kirkwall

MUTTON SOUP WITH DUMPLINGS

1½ lb boiling mutton,   4 carrots, grated
  chopped   2 onions, chopped
4 pints water   Salt and pepper
8 oz yellow split peas (soaked overnight)

METHOD

1. Boil the water, add the peas and mutton, simmer for one and a half hours, then skim.
2. Add the carrots, onions and seasoning, and simmer for a further three quarters of an hour.
3. Add the dumplings and cook for 20 minutes.

DUMPLINGS

8 oz flour   ½ teaspoon baking soda
1 tablespoon sugar   Milk to mix
½ teaspoon salt

METHOD

1. Mix all ingredients with milk to form a dough.
2. Divide the mixture into four equal parts.
3. Roll well in flour, and boil in soup for final 20 minutes.

M. Lyon, Stromness

FISH

SMOKED FISH SUPREME

Small quantity of butter
12 oz smoked fish
2 cups milk

Crustless slices of bread
4 oz cheese, grated
2 eggs

METHOD

1. Grease an 8-inch pie dish with butter.
2. Cover bottom and sides with slices of buttered bread.
3. Break fish into chunks and place on top of bread.
4. Cover fish with cheese.
5. Beat eggs and milk together and pour over contents.
6. Bake for 45 minutes in oven (350°), (mark 4).

J. Butcher, South Ronaldsay

BIRSAY HADDOCK SOUFFLE

1 oz margarine
1 oz flour
¼ pint milk

2 eggs, separated
1 haddock, boiled
Seasoning

METHOD

1. Skin and bone haddock then rub through a sieve.
2. Melt margarine in a pan and add flour.
3. Slowly add milk to make a thick sauce.
4. Remove from heat, add egg yolks, fish and seasoning.
5. Fold in stiffly beaten whites.
6. Bake for 25-30 minutes in oven (350°), (mark 4).

B. Coghill, Birsay

PENTLAND FIRTH PIE

¼ lb cooked cod   1 dessertspoon butter
½ lb mashed potatoes   Salt and pepper

METHOD

1. Skin, flake and remove bones from cod.
2. Melt butter in pan and add the potatoes (if too dry add a tablespoon of milk) and beat well with a fork.
3. Add the fish and season to taste. Heat thoroughly.
4. Put neatly into a pie dish and brown under the grill.

T. Robertson, Longhope

BAKED STUFFED BIRSAY COD

1 medium cod   2 oz lard

Stuffing

2 tablespoons breadcrumbs   Juice of 1 lemon with a
1 tablespoon chopped suet   little grated rind
½ tablespoon parsley, chopped Salt and pepper
1 egg to bind

Coating

Melted margarine and brown breadcrumbs.

METHOD

1. Wash fish and remove bones.
2. Prepare stuffing by mixing ingredients together and binding stiffly with beaten egg.
3. Press stuffing into centre of fish and tie into shape.
4. Brush with melted margarine and sprinkle with the breadcrumbs.
5. Place fish in melted lard in a baking tin and bake for 30 minutes in oven (350°), (mark 4), basting frequently.
6. Serve on a hot ashet garnished with parsley.

D. Taylor, Birsay

CASSEROLE OF SMOKED FISH

1 lb smoked fillets
1 oz margarine
1 oz flour
½ pint milk
Pepper to taste

¼ pint water
1 teaspoon finely
    chopped onion
1 tablespoon finely
    chopped ham

METHOD

1. Place the milk, water, onion, ham, margarine and pepper in a pan. Cover and simmer for 10 minutes.
2. Wash the fillets and cut them into neat pieces. Add to the mixture in the pan and simmer for 30 minutes.
3. Mix the flour to a smooth paste with a little milk. Add this to the mixture and stir to boil.
4. Serve with mashed potatoes and thin fingers of toast.

T. Foubister, Kirkwall

BAKED FILLETS WITH TOMATO SAUCE

8 fillets of sole
3 large tomatoes
1 onion

1 tablespoon milk
Tomato sauce
Seasoning

METHOD

1. Mix the chopped tomatoes and onion together.
2. Season the fillets, then spread the tomatoes and onion on them.
3. Fold the fillets over and place in a buttered baking dish with a tablespoon of milk, and bake in oven for 20 minutes (350°), (mark 4).
4. Serve with tomato sauce.

J. Leslie, Kirkwall

23

FISH CASSEROLE

¾ lb white fish fillets
1 large onion
3 tomatoes

2 oz margarine
¾ pint milk
Salt and pepper

METHOD

1. Place fillets in a greased casserole dish.
2. Slice onions into rings and place on top of fish.
3. Slice tomatoes and add along with seasoning.
4. Pour on milk and dot with margarine.
5. Bake for one hour in oven (350°), (mark 4). Scallops or clams may be used in place of fillets.

M. Davidson, Balfour

SOUSED HERRING

6 herrings
2 small onions, cut into rings
½ pint mixed vinegar and
  water

1 tablespoon mixed pickling
  spice
4 bay leaves
Salt and pepper

METHOD

1. Scale, clean and bone herrings.
2. Season well with salt and pepper.
3. Roll up and place fairly close together in an ovenproof dish.
4. Cover with vinegar and water.
5. Sprinkle with pickling spice.
6. Garnish with bay leaves and onion rings.
7. Cover with baking foil or lid and bake for 45 minutes in oven (350°), (mark 4).

H. Garson, Sandwich

ORKNEY SEASIDE CURRY

Limpets to fill a 6-pint pot   2 oz fat
2 teaspoons curry powder   4 oz rice

METHOD

1. Boil sufficient water to cover the limpets.
2. Add the limpets and boil until they come out of their shells.
3. Strain, cool and then remove the heads.
4. Mince limpets and fry in fat for a few minutes.
5. Add the curry powder and serve on bed of cooked rice.

M. Mainland, Birsay

DEVILLED LOBSTERS

1 large lobster   1 teaspoon Worcester
1 teaspoon chutney   sauce
1 oz butter   3 tablespoons white
½ teaspoon mustard   sauce
Salt   A dust of cayenne
Brown breadcrumbs

METHOD

1. Take all the meat from a large boiled lobster and cut into small pieces.
2. Pound the coral in a mortar with the mustard, butter and other flavourings.
3. Put the white sauce into a saucepan and add the pounded coral etc. to it.
4. Let it heat thoroughly, then stir in the lobster and bring it to boiling point.
5. Prepare buttered fireproof shells on a dish. Put the mixture into these, and sprinkle the top with brown breadcrumbs. Brown under the grill.
6. Garnish with fresh parsley to serve.

I. MacDonald, Kirkwall

CROFTERS' HOTPOT

4 large herring fillets
2 oz butter
2 large onions, sliced

4 medium potatoes, sliced
Salt and pepper

METHOD

1. Season fillets well and place half in a well-greased dish.
2. Cover fillets with onion slices then with potato slices.
3. Season and dab with butter.
4. Repeat layers, finishing with potatoes.
5. Season again and dab with butter.
6. Cover closely and bake for 50 minutes in oven (425°), (mark 6). Remove cover and bake for another 10 minutes.

Mrs Bleshe, Westray

ORKNEY TROUT CRUNCH

1 trout
1 oz butter
1 oz flour
1 large can evaporated milk
Seasoning

2 tablespoons lemon juice
½ stick finely chopped celery
4 oz breadcrumbs
2 oz melted butter

METHOD

1. Melt 1 oz butter in a pan and add flour.
2. Gradually stir in evaporated milk. Bring to the boil, stirring until thickened.
3. Flake trout, and add to sauce with lemon juice, celery and seasoning.
4. Mix well, and put into a greased 2-pint pie dish.
5. Mix breadcrumbs with melted butter and sprinkle on top.
6. Bake for 30 minutes in oven (350°), (mark 4). Alternatively, use a can of salmon.

H. Garson, Sandwick

SALMON PIE

½ tin salmon   2 oz margarine
1 teacup milk   2 eggs
1 teacup breadcrumbs   Salt and pepper

METHOD

1. Put milk and margarine into pan and heat slowly till margarine melts.
2. Add breadcrumbs.
3. Beat eggs.
4. Break up salmon with a fork.
5. Mix all ingredients together and put in a well-greased dish.
6. Bake for 30 minutes in oven (350°), (mark 4).
6. Serve with chips, or cold with salad.

J. Muir, Stenness

GRAEMSAY PARTAN

1 boiled partan (large crab)   1 tablespoon salad cream
1 hard-boiled egg finely grated Seasoning
2 tablespoons fresh
  breadcrumbs

METHOD

1. Pick all the meat from the boiled partan, discarding the stomach bag.
2. Place the meat in a bowl and add the egg, breadcrumbs, salad cream, and seasoning.
3. Mix together, and place on a bed of lettuce, garnished with tomatoes.
4. Serve with oatcakes.

M. Lyon, Stenness

FRICASSEE OF FISH

1 lb white fish	Parsley
1 shallot or small onion	Salt
	A blade of mace
1 pint milk	Pinch of cayenne
2 hard-boiled eggs	6 drops lemon juice
1 oz butter	Strip of lemon peel,
1 oz flour	one inch

METHOD

1. Boil the milk in a stewpan with the shallot, mace, cayenne and lemon peel.
2. Cut the fish into pieces 1½ inches square and simmer in the milk for 15 minutes. Remove the fish and keep it warm.
3. To prepare the sauce, melt the butter in a saucepan, add the flour, and fry without browning.
4. Strain the milk onto the butter, add a pinch of salt, and boil for 3 minutes stirring constantly.
5. Arrange the fish in the centre of a very hot dish. Take the sauce off the heat, add the lemon juice and pour it over the fish.
6. Cut the eggs into 8 pieces lengthways. Put 2 pieces on top of the fish with a sprig of parsley between, then form a border round the dish with the other pieces of egg, placing a sprig of parsley between each piece of egg.

P. Laird, Kirkwall

28

MEAT

HOME-BREW ORKNEY STEW

1 lb lean stewing steak	2 large onions
1 large kidney	¼ lb mushrooms
½ lb turnip	½ cup ground oatmeal
½ lb carrots	Home-brew ale
1 lb small scrubbed new	Bisto gravy
potatoes	Seasoned flour

METHOD

1. Heat a little oil in a stewing pan.
2. Roll pieces of meat and kidney in seasoned flour and seal in the hot oil.
3. Add sufficient home-brew ale to cover.
4. Bring to the boil and simmer gently for 75 minutes.
5. Add chopped carrots, turnip, onions and oatmeal. Return to the boil and simmer for another 15 minutes.
6. Add mushrooms and Bisto gravy and simmer for another 8 minutes before serving.

I. Thomson, Stromness

BEEFSTEAK AND KIDNEY PUDDING

2 lb steak	Vinegar
1½ lb suet paste	1 teaspoon parsley
1 ox kidney	Salt
1 shallot	Pepper

METHOD

1. Cut the beefsteak into pieces.
2. Cover the kidney with cold water, add a tablespoon of vinegar and let it soak for 10 minutes. Rinse it in cold water, dry it, core it and slice it.
3. Butter a pudding basin and line it with suet paste leaving a good margin hanging over the edge.
4. Put in a layer of the steak and kidney, sprinkle it with a

29

little of the chopped parsley, shallot, pepper and salt. Repeat the layers until the basin is full then pour in half a cup of cold water.

5. Cut out a piece of paste the size of the basin and lay it on top. Wet the edges, fold over the margin of paste lining and press down firmly.
6. Lay a buttered paper over the top, then a pudding cloth and tie it on firmly.
7. Put the pudding in a saucepan partly filled with boiling water and boil for 4 hours.
8. Turn the pudding out on to a hot dish and garnish with a little chopped parsley to serve.

B. Muir, Stromness

STEWED STEAK AND OYSTERS

1½ lb steak	½ wineglass Port wine
18 oysters	1 teaspoon flour
2 oz butter	½ pint water
1 onion	Pepper and salt

METHOD

1. Melt the butter in a stewpan. Slice the onion and fry it in the butter until it is golden brown.
2. Cut the steak into thick pieces and fry in the butter for 15 minutes.
3. Add the water and season to taste.
4. Add the liquor from the oysters, cover the pan, and let it simmer for 1 hour.
5. Mix the flour with the port wine and thicken the gravy.
6. Draw the pan from the heat, add the oysters and stir until they are plump. Do not let it boil.
7. Dish up the steak, put the oysters round, and pour on the gravy.
8. Garnish with croûtons of fried bread, brushed with white of egg and dipped in grated parmesan cheese.

J. Leslie, Kirkwall

BEEF OLIVES

Long thin steaks	Oil
1 glass white wine	Flour
Brown gravy	Butter
Cayenne	

Forcemeat

Breadcrumbs	Grated lemon peel
Beef suet, minced	Nutmeg
Parsley, chopped	Salt and pepper
Egg yolk	

METHOD

1. Mix all the ingredients together to prepare the forcemeat.
2. Spread a layer of the forcemeat over each steak, roll and tie with fine string.
3. Fry the olives lightly in oil, then add gravy, wine and a little cayenne. Thicken with a little flour and butter.
4. Cover tightly and stew for 1 hour. Remove string to serve.

P. Tulloch, Kirkwall

BAKED BEEF AND BACON LOAF

4 oz bacon, minced	1 teaspoon mixed herbs
8 oz raw beef, minced	A little stock
4 oz white breadcrumbs	Salt and pepper
1 onion	

METHOD

1. Mix bacon, beef and breadcrumbs together.
2. Finely chop onion and add to beef mixture with herbs and seasoning.
3. Moisten with a little stock and put into a greased loaf tin.
4. Cover with foil and bake for 2 hours in oven (350°) (mark 4).
5. Serve with jacket potatoes.

M. Tulloch, Sanday

BALFOUR BEEF

2 lb beef
1 lb bacon
1 lemon rind
2 egg yolks
½ teaspoon nutmeg

Pepper and salt
Thyme and parsley
Brown gravy
Fried potatoes

METHOD

1. Chop the beef finely, pass the bacon through the mincer twice and mix them together.
2. Finely chop the lemon rind and mix it with the parsley and thyme. Add the grated nutmeg and pepper and salt to taste. The quantity of salt must be according to the saltiness of the bacon.
3. Add all these ingredients to the chopped meat and mix them together with the egg yolks.
4. Form the mixture into a roll and wrap it in buttered paper and bind it with tape to keep it in shape. Put it in a well-greased baking tin, and bake in oven for 1-1½ hours (350°), (mark 4).
5. When cooked, remove the binding and paper, place the roll on a hot dish and pour on a rich brown gravy.
6. Garnish with fried potatoes to serve.

E. Miller, Kirkwall

WARD SPECIALITY

1 lb stewing steak, in a lump
2 onions
1 curry stock cube
Shake of chilli powder

4 carrots
12 oz rice
Oil

METHOD

1. Slice the steak very thinly and cut roughly into 2″ × 1″ pieces.
2. Fry quickly in the oil, browning the pieces thoroughly.

3. Add the onion, diced, and brown slightly.
4. Dissolve the stock cube in ¼-½ pint of water and add to frying pan along with seasoning, chilli and sliced carrots, and allow to simmer till carrots are cooked.
5. Serve on a bed of boiled rice.

L. Ward, Sanday

MUTTON CUTLETS WITH TOMATOES

6 mutton cutlets   Butter
8 medium tomatoes   Pepper
Mashed potatoes   Salt

METHOD

1. Cut the cutlets from the best end of a neck of mutton. Trim them neatly and scrape the end bone.
2. Put some butter on a plate and season it well with pepper and salt. Dip the cutlets in the seasoned butter and let them soak for an hour.
3. Submerge the tomatoes in boiling water and then skin them. Put them into a buttered baking dish, season with pepper, salt and a pinch of castor sugar. Lay a buttered paper over them to cook in oven for 15-20 minutes (350°), (mark 4).
4. Lay the cutlets on a grill and cook quickly.
5. Prepare mashed potatoes and arrange a straight line down the centre of a dish.
6. Place the cutlets down the centre of the potatoes letting one cutlet overlap another.
7. Arrange a border of tomatoes down each side.

P. Harcus, Kirkwall

c

GAIRSAY MUTTON

1 lb mutton	1 small turnip
1 oz flour	1 tomato
Spaghetti	Herbs
1 oz butter	1 pint weak stock
8 button onions	or water
2 small young	Pepper
carrots	Salt

METHOD

1. Cut the mutton into small pieces.
2. Melt the butter in a stewpan, then put in the meat, the onions and the sliced carrots and turnip. Fry until a golden colour, then stir in the flour.
3. Add the stock or water, pepper and salt to taste, and a bunch of savoury herbs tied up in muslin. Bring to the boil and skim well.
4. Reduce the heat, and simmer for 1-1½ hours.
5. Boil spaghetti in salted water with an onion, and make a border of it round the dish. Pour the ragoût into the centre.
6. Arrange a twist of spaghetti on the top and serve.

T. Mowat, Kirkwall

MUTTON FRITTERS

1 lb breast of mutton	1 large onion
1 carrot	Frying batter
1 small turnip	Frying fat
½ stick of celery	A bunch of herbs
Pepper and salt	(bayleaf, thyme
	and parsley)

METHOD

1. Clean and slice the vegetables and put them into a saucepan with the meat. Cover with cold water, bring to the boil and remove scum.

34

2. Simmer gently until the meat is tender.
3. Take the meat from the saucepan and lay it on a flat plate, sprinkle it with finely chopped parsley, onion and salt and pepper.
4. Put another flat dish on top with a weight on it and allow to stand until the meat is cold.
5. Cut the meat into fingers 2 inches by 1½ inches, dip them in frying batter and fry in hot fat until they are golden brown.
6. Arrange neatly on a hot dish and sprinkle a little chopped parsley on the top. Pour on Reform sauce to serve.

E. Miller, Kirkwall

STEWED BREAST OF LAMB

A breast of lamb	1½ pints green peas
White stock	Potato balls
2 oz butter	1 blade of mace
¾ oz flour	½ teaspoon white
1 teaspoon salt	pepper

METHOD

1. Cut the lamb into pieces and lay in a stewpan with a blade of mace, and sprinkle with a teaspoon of salt and ½ teaspoon of white pepper.
2. Add stock to cover, place the lid on the pan and simmer gently for 45 minutes. Skim well and remove the mace.
3. Add 1 pint of the peas and simmer for another 30 minutes.
4. Mix the butter and flour together and stir it into the gravy. Simmer for another 10 minutes.
5. Take out the pieces of meat and arrange on a dish. Pour on the sauce, garnish with potato balls, and the remaining ½ pint of peas, plainly boiled.

B. Muir, Stromness

PEEDIE PIES

1 lb lean mutton	Seasoning
1 onion	Flour to thicken
¼ lb mushrooms	¾ lb short crust pastry

METHOD

1. Chop the mutton, mushrooms and onion into small pieces.
2. Put the chopped mutton into a pan with sufficient water to cover and cook until tender.
3. Add the mushrooms and onion to the pan, season and cook for another ten minutes.
4. Thicken with flour and allow to cool.
5. Roll out the pastry and cut into rounds to line small bun tins, retaining enough pastry to make rounds to cover.
6. Spoon some of the mixture into each pastry case.
7. Cut a small hole in the centre of each pastry lid, place them in position and seal the edges.
8. Brush with egg, and bake until brown.

J. Watt, Stromness

BAKED ORKNEY HAM WITH BANANAS

3 slices Orkney ham ¾″ thick	½ cup flaked coconut
3 bananas, sliced	4 tablespoons lemon juice
½ cup brown sugar	2 tablespoons butter

METHOD

1. Cut the ham slices in half.
2. Arrange in a shallow greased baking tin and spread sliced bananas on top.
3. Sprinkle on the lemon juice, brown sugar and coconut.
4. Bake for 1 hour in oven (350°), (mark 4).

J. Flett, Orphir

Baskets of fresh crabs on Stromness Pier

Two lobsters fresh from the Pentland Firth

STENNESS HAM AND TOMATO PIE

5 oz shortcrust pastry
½ lb ham
2 small tomatoes
1 boiled potato
1 hard-boiled egg

2 oz Orkney cheese, grated
¼ pint milk
1 egg
Salt and pepper

METHOD

1. Line a dish with half the pastry.
2. Beat the egg with the milk and seasoning.
3. Chop ham, tomatoes, potato, and hard-boiled egg and place in dish, topped with grated cheese.
4. Pour in egg mixture and cover with other half of pastry.
5. Bake for 10 minutes in oven (375°), (mark 5), then lower heat and continue cooking for a further 30 minutes.

W. Reid, Stenness

BAKED SWEETBREADS

1 calf's sweetbread
1 beaten egg
Breadcrumbs

Gravy
Salt
1 oz butter

METHOD

1. Boil the sweetbread for 15 minutes in slightly salted water. Dry it, then cut it in half lengthwise.
2. Dip each half into the beaten egg, then into fine white breadcrumbs.
3. Butter a baking tin, lay the pieces in and bake in oven for 20 minutes (350°), (mark 4) basting them with the butter.
4. Lay the pieces side by side on a hot dish, pour on a brown gravy, and garnish with fried parsley to serve.

L. Grieve, Kirkwall

STRONSAY VEAL

1½ lbs cooked veal
½ lb cooked ham
2 onions
1 egg
Nutmeg
Pepper and salt

Butter
Sauce
One thick slice
  of bread
Milk

METHOD

1. Chop the veal and ham very finely.
2. Soak the bread in some milk.
3. Melt a little butter in a stewpan and fry the chopped onion until slightly brown.
4. Mix in the meat and the bread.
5. Add a large pinch of grated nutmeg, pepper and salt to taste. Stir until thoroughly mixed and heated.
6. Take the pan from the heat and stir in a well-beaten egg.
7. Butter a mould, press the mixture firmly in and bake in a moderate oven for 1 hour.
8. Turn it out and serve with German sauce.

I. MacDonald, Kirkwall

40

POULTRY AND GAME

COUNTRY-STYLE CHICKEN

1 chicken	4 peeled and chopped
1 onion	tomatoes
1 clove garlic	½ tin chopped pineapple
2 oz diced bacon	1 small tin button
2 oz butter	mushrooms
2 oz flour	½ teaspoon sage
1½ pints stock	Salt and pepper

METHOD

1. Cut chicken into 4 joints and brown in a pan with the butter and the clove of garlic.
2. Add the onion and bacon and fry lightly.
3. Sprinkle with flour and stir well.
4. Add the sage and seasoning then the stock. Cover with a lid, and cook gently for 25 minutes.
5. Just before cooked, add the tomatoes, the mushrooms, and the pineapple, with a little of the juice.
6. Serve with pieces of fried bread and potatoes.

H. Garson, Sandwich

CHICKEN STUFFED WITH MUSHROOMS

2 small spring chickens	3 oz single cream
4 oz mushrooms	1 teaspoon cornflour
4 oz butter	Chopped parsley
1 onion	Paprika

METHOD

1. Finely chop the onion and cook in half the butter for 5 minutes with the lid on the pan. Slice the mush-

41

rooms, add to the onions and cook for 4 minutes. Season and allow to cool.
2. Stuff the chickens with the mushroom mixture. Melt the rest of the butter in a fireproof dish and gently fry the chickens until brown. Season well, and pour over 2 tablespoons of water. Cook in oven for 20 minutes (350°), (mark 4).
3. When tender, remove from the casserole and split each bird in half. Arrange on a warm serving dish and put in a low oven while you prepare the sauce.
4. To make the sauce, mix the cream with the gravy in the casserole, bring slowly to the boil and season to taste. Add 2 tablespoons of cornflour to thicken.
5. Spoon the sauce over each bird and decorate with chopped parsley to serve.

T. Bews, Kirkwall

OYSTER CHICKEN

1 chicken	¼ lb butter
12 oysters	Flour
1 pint gravy	Seasoning
2 blades of mace	1 anchovy
½ sliced nutmeg	½ glass white wine
Sweet herbs	½ lemon

METHOD

1. Part-boil the chicken and cut the meat into small pieces. Stew in the gravy with the oysters, mace, nutmeg, herbs and seasoning.
2. When nearly done, take out the herbs, mace and nutmeg.
3. Add the butter, flour, chopped anchovy and wine.
4. Garnish with sliced lemon to serve.

K. Wilson, Stromness

CHICKEN BAKED IN RICE

1 chicken   Boiled rice
Slices of ham   Flour paste
1 pint gravy   Seasoning
1 onion, finely minced

METHOD

1. Line a pudding dish with slices of ham.
2. Cut the chicken into joints, season well, and lay them in the pudding dish.
3. Add the gravy and onion.
4. Fill the dish with boiled rice, well pressed and piled as high as possible.
5. Cover with a paste of flour and water and bake for 1 hour.
6. Remove the paste to serve.

J. Thomson, Stromness

SMOTHERED TURKEY

8 large slices cold turkey   ½ pint soured cream
¾ lb rice   Pinch of nutmeg
1½ oz butter   2 tablespoons chopped chives
1 onion, finely chopped   Seasoning

METHOD

1. Cook the rice in boiling salted water. Drain and rinse with hot water. Dry and put in the bottom of casserole dish.
2. Cover the rice with the slices of turkey. Cover with buttered paper and heat in oven for 20 minutes.
3. Melt the butter, and cook the finely chopped onion until tender but not brown. Add the soured cream, seasoning, and the pinch of nutmeg and mix well.
4. Spoon the soured cream sauce over the turkey and rice and sprinkle with chopped chives to serve.

J. Brown, Stromness

RABBIT HOTPOT

1 rabbit
¼ lb streaky bacon
4 onions
Small head of celery
Small white cabbage
6 potatoes

Stock or water
Flour
Pepper
Salt
Glass of red wine

METHOD

1. Divide the rabbit into joints. Dip the pieces into seasoned flour and brown in a frying-pan.
2. Place the rabbit in a casserole draped with the bacon.
3. Prepare and slice the vegetables and place around the rabbit.
4. Half fill the casserole with stock or water, pour on the wine and season well. Cover and cook in oven for 2½ hours (350°), (mark 4).

L. Cooper, Kirkwall

DUCK WITH RED CABBAGE

1 medium duck
1 small red cabbage
3 onions
2 tablespoons vinegar
2 tablespoons water
4 cooking apples

1 teaspoon sugar
2 tablespoons oil
1 teaspoon caraway seeds
¼ pint stock
1 tablespoon chopped parsley

METHOD

1. Braise the cabbage, then shred it very finely. Chop up one of the onions and mix it with the cabbage then place it in a well-buttered casserole. Add vinegar, water and seasoning. Cover, and cook in oven for 1 hour (350°), (mark 4). Add the sliced apples with a little sugar, and cook for another 15 minutes.
2. Cut the duck into 4 pieces. Heat the oil, and brown the

pieces of duck all over. Now place the duck on top of the cabbage in the casserole.

3. Cook the 2 remaining sliced onions in the remaining oil until just soft. Sprinkle in the caraway seeds and add a little stock. Add seasoning, and pour over the pieces of duck. Return to the oven for 40 minutes until tender.

4. Scrape the onion mixture off the duck and mix well into the cabbage. Arrange the pieces of duck on top of the cabbage and sprinkle with chopped parsley.

5. Serve hot with mashed potatoes and redcurrant jelly.

N. Bruce, Kirkwall

PIGEONS WITH RICE AND PARMESAN CHEESE

3 pigeons
Butter
Flour
2 pints stock
2 onions, grated
Seasoning
1 egg, beaten

Juice of 1 lemon
½ lb rice
Nutmeg, grated
Salt
½ cup grated Parmesan
  cheese

METHOD

1. Clean the pigeons and cut them into quarters.

2. Brown some of the butter with flour and add 1 pint of stock, the grated onions and seasoning. Stew the pigeons until tender.

3. Take out the pigeons and add the lemon juice to the stock, bring to the boil, and strain over the pigeons.

4. Boil the rice in 1 pint of stock with a knob of butter, some grated nutmeg and salt. When the rice is cooked, dry it and add half the Parmesan cheese.

5. Put half the rice round the dish, place the pigeons in the dish and cover with the remains of the rice. Pour over the egg, and sprinkle over the rest of the cheese.

6. Bake for 45 minutes in oven (300°) (mark 2). It should be a fine golden colour when ready.

W. Tait, Kirkwall

WARDHILL PIE

1 rabbit	8 oz flour
1 onion	1 tablespoon baking powder
2 oz grated raw potato	Salt and pepper
2 oz suet	

METHOD

1. Wash the rabbit in salted water and cut into neat joints.
2. Mix the flour with the baking powder, salt and suet.
3. Add the grated potato and mix to a dry dough with very little water.
4. Roll out thinly, and use two thirds of the dough to line a greased pudding bowl.
5. Put the rabbit into the bowl with the onion, a few diced potatoes and seasoning.
6. Add a little stock and cover with remaining pastry dough.
7. Cover with greaseproof paper and steam for 2 hours.

T. Robertson, Longhope

GAME PIE

2 grouse	½ pint red wine
½ lb steak	½ pint stock
½ lb streaky bacon	1 egg
1 large onion	Puff pastry
6 mushrooms	Pinch of nutmeg
2 tablespoons chopped herbs	Seasoning

METHOD

1. Cut the meat off the grouse, cut the steak and bacon into small pieces. Arrange in a pie-dish in layers with finely chopped onion, mushrooms, herbs and seasoning between each layer.
2. Pour on the red wine and enough stock to barely cover

the meat. Cover with foil and bake slowly in oven for
1-1½ hours (325°), (mark 3) until the meat is tender.
Allow to cool.
3. Roll out the pastry, cut a strip, moisten it, and place it
   round the edge of the dish. Moisten the top of the
   strip, and place a large piece of pastry on top and
   press the edges together. Cut off any surplus and crimp
   the edges. Slash the top of the pastry to release steam
   and decorate with pastry leaves.
4. Bake in oven for 30 minutes (425°), (mark 7).

J. Chalmers, Stromness

TURKEY CUTLETS

6 oz turkey	1 egg
1 oz butter	2 oz flour
1 onion, chopped	2 eggs beaten with 1 teaspoon
6 oz mashed potatoes	oil
1 teaspoon mixed herbs	6 oz white breadcrumbs
2 tablespoons chutney	Fat to fry
Tomato sauce	

METHOD

1. Chop the turkey. Melt the butter and cook the onion
   until tender.
2. Add the onion to the turkey with enough mashed
   potato to make a firm mixture, stirring in the herbs,
   chutney, beaten egg and seasoning.
3. Mould the mixture into cutlet shapes, and roll in
   seasoned flour. Brush with eggs beaten in oil and cover
   with dry breadcrumbs.
4. Heat fat and fry cutlets for a few minutes until golden
   brown, drain and serve with tomato sauce.

E. Johnston, Stromness

RABBIT WITH MUSTARD SAUCE

2 rabbits
Seasoned flour
2 oz butter
¼ lb streaky bacon, chopped
2 large onions, chopped

1 teaspoon dried herbs
¼ pint dry white wine
¼ pint stock
4 teaspoons Scotch mustard
½ pint double Orkney cream

METHOD

1. Joint the rabbits and coat with seasoned flour. Brown with the bacon in the melted butter.
2. Add the onions, herbs, wine and stock. Simmer gently until tender.
3. Strain the stock from the rabbit and keep the pieces warm in the oven in a serving dish.
4. Thoroughly mix the mustard into the fresh cream, add to the stock and season to taste.
5. Pour the sauce over the rabbit pieces to serve.

P. Anderson, Kirkwall

TURKEY AND ASPARAGUS

1½ cups diced turkey
1 cup hot white sauce
1½ cups hot boiled rice

1 tin asparagus
¼ cup mayonnaise

METHOD

1. Chop the asparagus into 1-inch pieces.
2. Grease a shallow casserole dish and arrange half the turkey in a layer. Cover with the asparagus and top with the rest of the turkey.
3. Stir the mayonnaise into the white sauce, allow it to cool, then spoon it over the turkey.
   Bake uncovered in a hot oven for 20-30 minutes. Serve with rice.

48

SAVOURY

NORTH ISLES SAVOURY

4 hard-boiled eggs
1 lb cold boiled potatoes
Chopped chives

1 pint of white sauce
3 oz grated cheese

METHOD

1. Slice the eggs and potatoes and arrange in layers in an ovenproof dish.
2. Sprinkle each layer with chives.
3. Pour white sauce over the last layer and cover the top with grated cheese.
4. Bake for 20 minutes in oven (400°), (mark 6).

R. Wallace, Shapinsay

LYONNAISE EGGS

6 eggs
1½ cups milk
1 chopped onion
1 tablespoon flour

½ cup breadcrumbs
2 tablespoons butter
Salt and pepper

METHOD

1. Cook the onion in the butter for 10 minutes. Add the flour, and cook until the mixture is smooth, stirring constantly.
2. Gradually pour in the milk, and cook for 3 minutes, stirring constantly.
3. Season with pepper and salt, and pour into a deep, hot baking dish.
4. Carefully break the 6 eggs into the mixture. Cover the eggs with the breadcrumbs.
5. Bake in oven for 10 minutes (350°), (mark 4).

E. Harvey, Stromness

D

TOASTED GIANTS

1 lb potatoes, boiled
4 eggs, hard boiled
2 medium onions, chopped
3 slices white bread

½ pint white sauce
1 oz white breadcrumbs
Seasoning

METHOD

1. Slice potatoes and eggs, and arrange in layers in a round, shallow pyrex dish and season well.
2. Stir chopped onions into hot, white sauce and add seasoning.
3. Pour the onion sauce over the egg and potato and sprinkle with breadcrumbs.
4. Bake for 30 minutes in oven (325°), (mark 4) until golden brown.
5. Cut each slice of bread in half and toast lightly.
6. Cut the toasted pieces into the shape of standing stones and stand upright round the dish to serve.

G. Sinclair, Stromness

WINTER SUPPER

1½ lbs potatoes
1 large Spanish onion,
  chopped
8 oz can of peeled tomatoes
3 slices corned beef

4 oz Orkney cheese, grated
2 oz Orkney butter
Seasoning

METHOD

1. Boil potatoes and mash with butter.
2. Fry the onion in a little oil until light brown.
3. Strain the tomatoes and discard the juice. Add the tomatoes to the onions in the frying pan, and mix to heat.
4. Arrange layers in deep oven dish, potato, cheese, corned beef, onion, tomato, finishing with potato, with cheese sprinkled on top.
5. Bake for 20 minutes in oven (350°), (mark 4).

J. Leslie, Kirkwall

HAM TOAST

8 tablespoons lean ham   Butter
2 egg yolks   Cayenne
6 tablespoons cream   Toast

METHOD

1. Take the lean remains of a ham, and chop finely.
2. To 8 tablespoons of ham add the yolks of 2 eggs well beaten, the cream, a piece of butter about the size of an egg, and a seasoning of cayenne pepper.
3. Stir over a moderate heat until the mixture begins to thicken.
4. Spread on squares of toast and serve very hot.

L. Flett, Orphir

MAESHOWE BACON SAVOURY

1 lb leeks, sliced   ¼ lb mushrooms
1 can baked beans   2 hard-boiled eggs
8 rashers bacon   1 tomato
¼ lb brussels sprouts   Butter for frying

METHOD

1. Fry the bacon rashers and keep hot in a dish.
2. Melt butter in the pan, add leeks and mushrooms, and fry until tender. Keep them hot in a dish.
3. Stir baked beans into fat in pan and heat well.
4. Boil the brussels sprouts.
5. To serve, heap the beans into the middle of a serving dish and top with sprouts rolled up in rashers of bacon. Heap leeks and mushrooms all around.
6. Garnish with slices or wedges of egg and fried tomato.

L. Mathers, Stenness

POTATO AND CHEESE MOULD

½ lb cooked potatoes
2 oz grated cheese
2 tablespoons milk or cream
1 oz melted butter

2 eggs, separated
A few browned breadcrumbs
Pepper and salt

METHOD

1. Sieve the potatoes and add the melted butter, the yolks of the eggs, the cheese, seasoning, and the milk or cream.
2. Whip the whites to a stiff froth and stir them lightly into the mixture.
3. Grease a mould or bowl, and line it with the bread-crumbs.
4. Pour in the mixture and bake for 30 minutes in oven (350°), (mark 4).
5. Turn out on to a hot dish to serve.

F. Kent, Westray

CHEESE, ONION AND POTATO PIE

8 oz potatoes
½ an onion
3 oz cheese
1 oz margarine

2½ fluid oz milk
Salt and pepper
Chopped parsley
4 eggs

METHOD

1. Boil potatoes.
2. Chop onion finely and fry until golden brown using half the margarine.
3. Drain the potatoes, add salt, pepper, milk, and the rest of the margarine and mash well.
4. Add the onion, a little parsley, and all but 2 table-

spoons of the cheese. Mix well and place in a warm, ovenproof dish.

5. Make 4 hollows in the mixture with the back of a spoon.
6. Drop an egg into each hollow and put a dot of butter on top of each one.
7. Sprinkle the grated cheese between the eggs.
8. Bake for 15 minutes in oven (375°), (mark 5) until the eggs set.

J. Sinclair, Sanday

STUFFED BACON ON TOAST

½ cup dry breadcrumbs
Lambs kidney
Beaten egg
10 slices bacon

½ small onion, chopped
½ tablespoon parsley
Salt
Pepper

METHOD

1. Mix the crumbs with the chopped onion, add parsley and seasoning, moisten with beaten egg, then spread the mixture on slices of bacon.
2. Fasten each slice round a piece of lamb's kidney with small skewers.
3. Bake in oven for 20 minutes (375°), (mark 5).
4. Serve on rounds of hot toast with the crusts removed. Garnish with halved tomatoes, baked or grilled, sprinkled with breadcrumbs, pepper and salt, and dabs of butter.

J. Flett, Kirkwall

ORKNEY BACON SAVOURY

½ lb bacon, minced
¼ lb mushrooms, chopped
3 tomatoes, sliced
1 onion, chopped

2 beaten eggs
½ lb grated cheese
4 oz breadcrumbs
2 oz margarine

METHOD

1. Add the minced bacon and chopped onion to the beaten egg and beat again.
2. Mix the cheese and breadcrumbs together.
3. Grease a casserole and put in layers, half the bacon mixture, half the mushrooms, half the tomatoes, and half the cheese and breadcrumbs mixture.
4. Repeat the layers again in the same order.
5. Put dabs of margarine on the top and bake for 30 minutes in oven (400°), (mark 6).

E. Slater, Kirkwall

HAMNAVOE PIE

4 oz shortcrust pastry
4 oz cooked chicken
2 oz gammon

4 oz chopped mushroom
2 eggs
Salt and pepper

METHOD

1. Line an 8-inch sandwich tin with the pastry.
2. Chop the chicken and gammon and lay in the pastry.
3. Sprinkle the mushroom over the top.
4. Beat the eggs, season and pour over the mixture.
5. Bake in oven for 20 minutes (350°), (mark 4) until eggs are set.

Oakleigh Hotel, Stromness

SCOTCH NIPS

6 oz cooked dried haddock   1 tablespoon double cream
2 egg yolks   White pepper and salt

METHOD

1. Chop up the fish and place it in a stew-pan.
2. Add the cream, egg yolks, pepper and salt to taste, and stir over a moderate heat till the mixture thickens.
3. Pile it on fried croûtes, sprinkle with a little paprika and serve hot.

J. Flett, Kirkwall

CHEESY MACARONI

½ lb macaroni   4 oz grated cheese
¾ lb mince   1 onion, finely chopped
2 oz tomato puree   1 packet tomato soup

METHOD

1. Cook the mince and onion.
2. Add the tomato puree.
3. Make the soup using only half the quantity of water recommended then add this to the mince.
4. Cook the macaroni.
5. Grease a dish and layer the mince and macaroni until all the ingredients are used, ending with a layer of macaroni.
6. Sprinkle the grated cheese on top.
7. Bake for 20 minutes in oven (350°), (mark 4) then brown under the grill.

M. Butcher, South Ronaldsay

RICE WITH CHEESE SAUCE

2 pints boiled rice
¼ cup grated Orkney cheese
¼ lb chopped fried
   mushrooms

½ pint white sauce
Paprika to taste

METHOD

1. Boil the rice in salted water. drain well, then rinse it under the cold tap in a collander. Drain well and add it to the white sauce.
2. Season to taste with paprika, add the cheese and the mushrooms and heat until the cheese has melted, stirring lightly. Serve at once.

L. Flett, Orphir

KIPPERED EGGS

2 kippers
1 oz margarine
2 tablespoons milk

2 eggs
Salt and pepper
Buttered toast

METHOD

1. Boil the kippers until tender.
2. When cold, remove the bones and flake the flesh.
3. Put into pan with margarine, milk, and lightly beaten eggs. Season lightly.
4. Cook gently, stirring constantly until eggs thicken.
5. Serve on buttered toast.

H. Garson, Sandwick

HADDOCK KEDGEREE

2 smoked haddocks
8 oz boiled rice
4 oz butter

2 hard-boiled eggs
Cayenne pepper
A few chopped mushrooms

METHOD

1. Melt the butter in a pan and cook the mushrooms. Add the flaked fish, rice and pepper and heat thoroughly.
2. Serve garnished with rings of egg white and the chopped yolks sprinkled over the top.

N. Wylie, Kirkwall

STUFFED CABBAGE

1 small cabbage
4 oz lard
1 onion

3 cups porage oats
Salt and pepper
Knob of butter

METHOD

1. Keep the outside leaves of the cabbage but shred the rest of it.
2. Cut up onion and brown in fat.
3. When the onion is brown, add the oats, salt and pepper, and fry until brown.
4. Grease steamer and put butter in the bottom.
5. Put oat mixture in steamer in layers with shredded cabbage.
6. Cover with cabbage leaves and steam for 1-1½ hours.

L. Mathers, Stenness

TROUT TOAST

A plump trout   Seasoning
White sauce   Cream
Lemon juice   Raw onion

METHOD

1. Boil the trout and flake the flesh into a bowl.
2. Make a little white sauce, add the flaked fish and season to taste. A little lemon juice may be added if desired.
3. Add a tablespoon of cream, mix well, and serve on hot buttered wholemeal bread garnished with a sprinkling of chopped raw onion.

L. Grieve, Kirkwall

ORKNEY CHEESE

8 pints full cream milk   1 teaspoon of rennet

METHOD

1. Heat the milk till lukewarm (about 85°F.)
2. Add the rennet with a little cold water and stir for a few minutes.
3. Let it stand for about 30 minutes until it becomes a firm curd, then break it up with a knife.
4. Repeat the procedure then strain through muslin.
5. Gently break up the curd with your fingers, add a little salt, and mix well.
6. Place the cheese in a chessit (cheese press) with a cloth underneath and a cloth on top. Place the lid in position and put on a 7-lb weight.
7. Take the cheese out and turn it for the next 8 days. Replace with a clean cloth each time.
8. Increase the weight after the first 2 days.
9. After the pressing is complete, dry it off at an open window.

F. Marian McNeill

VEGETABLES AND SALADS

CARROTS IN LEMON BUTTER

1 lb carrots	½ lemon
Butter	Salt

METHOD

1. Cut carrots into 3-inch lengths, quarter, and chop into pieces about a quarter of an inch thick.
2. Melt a large knob of butter in a saucepan and add the juice of half a lemon.
3. Simmer the carrots for 10 minutes.
4. Drain on kitchen towel and serve crisp.

E. Shaw, Kirkwall

NEW CARROTS AND CREAM

1 bundle of new carrots	1 tablespoon cream
1 oz butter	Pepper
1 egg yolk	Salt

METHOD

1. Boil the carrots in salted water for 20-30 minutes until tender.
2. Drain well, take them in a coarse cloth and rub gently to remove the skins.
3. Return to the saucepan with the butter and the pepper and salt. Beat up the egg yolk with the cream, and stir this mixture into the carrots until it thickens.
4. Arrange the carrots in a hot dish, and pour on the sauce to serve.

T. Foubister, Kirkwall

PURÉE OF TURNIPS

3 lb turnips	4 egg whites
4 tablespoons cream	Parsley
1 oz butter	Salt
2 tablespoons sifted flour	Pepper

METHOD

1. Pare and slice the turnips. Put them into a saucepan of cold water, with half a teaspoon of salt. Bring to the boil, strain, and rinse in cold water.
2. Now put the slices into fast-boiling salted water and boil until tender.
3. Drain well, dry on kitchen towel, and rub through a sieve.
4. Put this purée into a saucepan with the butter, half the cream, white pepper and salt, and sift in the flour. Stir with a wooden spoon until the mixture boils.
5. Butter a deep fireproof dish and put the purée into it, and pour on 2 tablespoons of cream.
6. Add a pinch of salt to the 4 egg whites and whip until stiff. Spread on top of the turnip purée.
7. Stand the dish in a tin of boiling water, and place it in a moderate oven until the egg turns golden brown.
8. Sprinkle with finely chopped parsley to serve.

P. Harcus, Kirkwall

BAKED MUSHROOMS

12 mushrooms	Salt
2 oz butter	Pepper

METHOD

1. Choose large, flat mushrooms. Wipe them with a clean cloth, peel them, and cut off the stalks close up to the crowns. Do not wash them unless absolutely necessary.
2. Butter a fireproof dish and lay the mushrooms edge to

60

edge dark side up. Sprinkle with pepper and salt and
put a small piece of butter on each one.
3. Cook in oven for 20 minutes (350°), (mark 4).
4. Serve piled on a hot dish and pour on the gravy which
has run from them.

T. Gorn, Kirkwall

LEEKS IN WHITE SAUCE

4 leeks   White sauce

METHOD

1. Trim off the roots, the outsides, and most of the green.
2. Slit leaves down a little way from the top and wash
thoroughly.
3. Place in a saucepan of boiling salted water for 30
minutes until tender.
4. Drain well, halve, and arrange in a hot dish. Serve with
white sauce. Leeks may also be stewed in brown gravy.

T. Gorn. Kirkwall

AUBERGINE FRITTERS

1 aubergine   Frying batter
Salt   Frying fat

METHOD

1. Peel a medium-sized aubergine and cut it in slices
about ½ inch thick. Soak in salt water for 30 minutes
then drain thoroughly.
2. Dip the pieces into frying batter, and fry in boiling fat
for 5 minutes. Drain on a wire pastry rack.
3. Pile on a hot dish and sprinkle on a little cayenne
pepper to serve.

L. Grieve, Kirkwall

61

TOMATO AU GRATIN

1 lb tomatoes
4 oz breadcrumbs
2 oz butter
1 teaspoon chopped shallot

1 teaspoon pepper
1 teaspoon salt
½ teaspoon castor sugar
4 oz grated cheese

METHOD

1. Scald and skin the tomatoes, then cut them in slices.
2. Butter a pie-dish, and line it thickly with buttered breadcrumbs.
3. Put in a layer of tomatoes, sprinkle with pepper, salt, sugar, cheese and a little finely chopped shallot. Cover with a layer of breadcrumbs, tomato, etc., until the dish is full. Finish with a layer of well-buttered breadcrumbs on top.
4. Bake in oven for 30 minutes (375°), (mark 5).

L. Allan, Stromness

BAKED TOMATOES

Tomatoes (2 per person)
Butter

Salt
Pepper

METHOD

1. Cut out the stalks from the tomatoes.
2. Butter a baking dish, and stand the tomatoes stalk end upwards.
3. Sprinkle seasoning into the hole left by the stalk and add a small piece of butter.
4. Lay a well-buttered paper on top and bake in a moderate oven for 10-15 minutes.

T. Foubister, Kirkwall

STOVIES

1 lb potatoes
Beef dripping or butter

Remains of a brisket of beef
Salt and pepper

METHOD

1. Peel and cut the potatoes into ¼-inch slices.
2. Boil a little salted water in a pan and simmer the potatoes until cooked.
3. Dry the potatoes and stir in sufficient beef dripping or butter until they are nicely coated.
4. Shred the ends of the brisket and stir into the potatoes. Season to taste.
5. Serve with oatcakes.

L. Drever, Stromness

CLAPSHOT

Potatoes
Turnip
Carrot
Chives

Butter
Salt
Pepper

METHOD

1. Boil equal quantities of potatoes, carrot and turnip. Finely chop the chives.
2. Drain and dry the potatoes, carrot and turnip and mash together with a generous knob of butter. Season well.
3. Sprinkle with the chives to serve.

L. Drever, Stromness

63

TATTIES 'N CREAM

2 lb new potatoes
4 oz butter
1 onion, chopped
1 cup single cream

Parsley, chopped
Mint, chopped
Seasoning

METHOD

1. Boil the potatoes in their skins, drain, peel and dice.
2. Melt the butter in a pan and add the onion, parsley, mint and seasoning. Stew until the onion is cooked. Mix in the potatoes and the cream.
3. Stir until the mixture boils then serve garnished with parsley.

J. Harcus, Westray

CABBAGE IN TOMATO SAUCE

1 white cabbage
1 chopped onion
14 oz tin tomatoes

½ cup olive oil
Mixed herbs
Seasoning

METHOD

1. Quarter the cabbage and cut out the stalk. Blanch in boiling salted water for 5 minutes then drain.
2. Cook the onion in the oil then add the tomatoes, seasoning and herbs.
3. Put the cabbage into the sauce, cover, and simmer until ready.

W. Harvey, Stromness

CREAMED BEETROOT

20 small beetroots, cooked
   and peeled
½ pint single cream
Chopped chives

2 oz Orkney smoked cheese,
   grated
1 oz Orkney butter

METHOD

1. Put the beetroot into a buttered oven-dish.
2. Pour on the cream and sprinkle with cheese, chives, seasoning and dot with knobs of butter.
3. Bake in a hot oven for 15 minutes.

W. Wylie, Kirkwall

ORANGE APPLE CHEESE

2 apples   4 oz Orkney cheese
2 oranges

METHOD

1. Peel and core the apples and cut into small pieces.
2. Peel and skin the oranges, divide into segments, and cut each segment into 4 pieces.
3. Roughly grate the cheese and mix with the fruit in a bowl to serve.

S. Croy, Kirkwall

POTATO SALAD

Potatoes   Mayonnaise
Onion   Parsley

METHOD

1. Chop the potato into small pieces and boil in salted water until just cooked.
2. Dry the potato and stir in sufficient mayonnaise to bind.
3. Finely chop the raw onion and mix into the potato.
4. Garnish with parsley to serve.

S. Croy, Kirkwall

E

TOMATO AND PEACH

6 tomatoes   Seasoning
8 oz tin of peach slices   Olive oil
Lemon juice

METHOD

1. Peel and slice the tomatoes. Drain the peaches and mix with the tomato.
2. Season with salt and pepper, sprinkle with a little lemon juice and olive oil to serve.

J. Watt, Kirkwall

PEACH COLESLAW

½ medium cabbage   ½ cup of sultanas
6 oz tin of peaches   Mayonnaise

METHOD

1. Soak the sultanas in warm water for 30 minutes.
2. Finely chop the cabbage and the peaches. Save the peach juice in a cup.
3. Mix the cabbage, peaches and sultanas together with sufficient mayonnaise to bind.
4. Before serving, pour on the juice of the peaches.

J. Watt, Kirkwall

EGG AND TOMATO

1. An equal amount of hard-boiled egg and tomato mixed to bind with mayonnaise is an ideal addition to a party cold table.

P. Dennison, Kirkwall

Mrs Harvey of Birsay applying the press to a batch of home-made cheese.

Packing Orkney butter at the Claymore Creamery in Kirkwall.

SAUCES

SIMPLE WHITE SAUCE

1 tablespoon butter or margarine	½ pint hot milk
1 tablespoon flour	Salt

METHOD

1. Melt the butter in a saucepan over a low heat.
2. Remove from the heat and blend in the flour and salt.
3. Return to heat and cook for 3 minutes without browning, stirring constantly.
4. Remove from the heat and gradually add the hot milk stirring constantly.
5. Return to the heat and cook for another five minutes, stirring constantly until the mixture is smooth and thickened.
6. Blend in a little chopped parsley to serve on fish or vegetables.

BROWN SAUCE

1 tablespoon butter or margarine	½ pint boiling water
1 tablespoon flour	Sprig of parsley
1 stock cube (beef)	Small bay leaf
	Pinch of dried thyme

METHOD

1. Melt the butter in a saucepan over a low heat.
2. Add the flour and cook for 6 minutes until medium brown.
3. Dissolve the oxo cube in the boiling water and gradually add to the mixture, stirring constantly until thickened and smooth.
4. Add the parsley, bay leaf and thyme and cook over a low heat for 20 minutes stirring occasionally.
5. Strain through a fine-mesh sieve to serve on meat.

ONION SAUCE

1½ cups finely chopped
onions
2 tablespoons butter
or margarine

2 cups hot white
sauce
½ cup double cream

METHOD

1. Cover onion with boiling water and stand for 3 minutes.
2. Melt the butter in a saucepan over a low heat.
3. Drain the onion and cook in the melted butter for 5 minutes until soft.
4. Stir into white sauce and simmer for 15 minutes, stirring occasionally.
5. Strain and gradually stir in the cream.
6. Serve with fish, poultry or vegetables.

BROWN MUSHROOM SAUCE

¼ cup sliced mushroom
caps (reserve stems)
3 cups water
½ medium onion
½ stalk celery,
sliced
½ carrot, sliced

1 parsley sprig
1 tablespoon butter
or margarine
1½ cups hot brown
sauce
1 teaspoon minced
fresh parsley

METHOD

1. Place mushroom stems in saucepan; add water, onion, celery, carrot and sprig of parsley.
2. Simmer over a low heat for 30 minutes.
3. Strain and measure broth. There should be three quarters of a cup.
4. Melt butter over low heat.
5. Add sliced mushrooms and cook until tender.
6. Stir in brown sauce.
7. Place over boiling water and heat for 15 minutes.
8. Stir in mushroom stock and minced parsley.
9. Serve with meat and poultry.

APPLE SAUCE

1 lb cooking apples   2 tablespoons water
½ oz butter   1 teaspoon sugar
                               (if required)

METHOD

1. Peel and core the apples and slice them thinly.
2. Put them into a saucepan with the water, cover and cook
   gently until they turn to a pulp.
3. Beat the pulp with a wooden spoon and add the butter
   and sugar to taste.
4. Serve on roast pork.

BREAD SAUCE

½ pint milk   6 peppercorns
2 oz fine white   Small blade of mace
  breadcrumbs   Cayenne pepper
1 oz butter   1 tablespoon cream
1 small onion, chopped
2 cloves

METHOD

1. Put the milk into a saucepan with the onion, cloves,
   peppercorns, mace and a little cayenne and bring it
   almost to the boil.
2. Take the pan off the heat and allow the ingredients to
   fuse for 15 minutes.
3. Strain the milk on to the breadcrumbs and add the
   butter.
4. Bring the sauce to the boil and add salt to taste.
5. Finally stir in a tablespoon of cream.

71

GERMAN SAUCE

2 oz flour
2 oz butter
3 egg yolks

Lemon juice
1 pint white stock

METHOD

1. Melt 1½ oz butter in a saucepan. Stir in the flour and cook for 3 minutes stirring constantly.
2. Gradually stir in 1 pint of well-flavoured white stock until it boils, then let it cook for 10 minutes.
3. Beat the egg yolks in a basin and pour the boiling sauce on to them, stirring all the time.
4. Add a few drops of lemon juice, the remainder of the butter, and serve.

REFORM SAUCE

2 oz flour
1 oz butter
2 oz tomatoes
1 small onion
1 pint of brown
  stock
Pepper and salt

1 tablespoon red
  currant jelly
2 tablespoons Port
  wine
A few drops lemon
  juice

METHOD

1. Melt the butter in a saucepan. Add the onion, finely chopped and fry till golden brown.
2. Add the flour and fry until a rich brown.
3. Slice the tomatoes and add them to the above ingredients together with a pint of brown stock. Stir together until it boils and simmer for 45 minutes, then stir in the red currant jelly, wine, lemon juice and the seasoning.
4. Rub the mixture through a fine sieve and re-heat to serve.

MINT SAUCE

2 tablespoons chopped
  mint
Boiling water

1 dessertspoon sugar
2 tablespoons brown
  vinegar

METHOD

1. Chop the mint very finely.
2. Melt the sugar with one tablespoon of boiling water in
   the sauce-boat, add the mint and vinegar.
3. Serve cold on roast lamb.

MUSTARD SAUCE

1 onion
1 oz butter or
  margarine
1 teaspoon dry
  English mustard

½ pint vinegar
½ oz flour
¼ pint water

METHOD

1. Finely chop the onion and fry in the butter until light
   brown.
2. Add the flour, then mustard, vinegar and water.
3. Bring to the boil and simmer for 12 minutes stirring
   frequently.

HORSERADISH SAUCE

1 teaspoon mustard
1 teaspoon vinegar
3 teaspoons cream

Salt
Horseradish, grated

METHOD

Mix the mustard, vinegar and cream together. Add a little
salt, and as much grated horseradish as will make a fairly
thick consistency.

HOLLANDAISE SAUCE

4 egg yolks
6 oz butter or
  margarine
½ cup boiling water

2 tablespoons lemon
  juice
½ teaspoon salt
Few grains cayenne
  pepper

METHOD

1. Place egg yolks in the top of a double boiler and beat slightly.
2. Heat butter in a saucepan until just melted then gradually blend into the egg yolks.
3. Gradually stir in the boiling water.
4. Cook until thickened, stirring constantly.
5. Remove from the heat and stir in the lemon juice, salt and cayenne.
6. Serve with vegetables, baked or broiled fish, and shellfish.

MOCK OYSTER SAUCE

3 anchovies, chopped
1 cup cream
Butter
Flour

¼ pint water
Mace
Cloves

METHOD

1. Simmer the anchovies in the water with a little mace and one or two cloves until anchovies dissolve.
2. Strain the mixture, and when it is quite cool, add the cream. Re-heat and thicken with a little butter and flour.
3. To be served on boiled fowl or veal.

CUSTARD SAUCE

½ pint milk   2 dessertspoons sugar
2 egg yolks, beaten   Vanilla essence

METHOD

1. Heat the milk and pour on to the beaten yolks then strain back into the rinsed pan.
2. Stir over a gentle heat until the mixture thickens but do not boil.
3. Add the sugar and the vanilla essence and mix well.

CHOCOLATE SAUCE

3 oz chocolate   ½ cup water
1 cup icing sugar   1 teaspoon vanilla essence
1 cup evaporated milk

METHOD

1. Cut the chocolate into small pieces and melt in a double boiler.
2. Stir in the sugar, milk and water. Stir until the sugar has dissolved and the mixture is perfectly blended.
3. Cook slowly for 10 minutes and flavour with vanilla to serve.

LEMON SAUCE

1 oz butter   3 dessertspoons sugar
2 dessertspoons cornflour   ½ pint water
Grated rind and juice of 1 lemon

METHOD

1. Melt the butter in a saucepan.
2. Mix the lemon rind, juice and water into the cornflour.
3. Add the mixture and the sugar to the melted butter and stir well. Bring to the boil and cook for 3 minutes.

MARMALADE SAUCE

½ pint water
Juice and rind of 1 lemon
2 dessertspoons cornflour

3 dessertspoons marmalade
1 dessertspoon sugar

METHOD

1. Put the water and the grated lemon rind into a saucepan and bring slowly to the boil.
2. Mix the lemon juice into the cornflour, add the marmalade and the sugar then the boiling liquid.
3. Return the mixture to the pan for 3 minutes until it thickens.

BUTTERSCOTCH SAUCE

2 oz butter
3 oz granulated sugar
2½ oz demerara sugar

1 cup golden syrup
Pinch of salt
½ cup double cream

METHOD

1. With the exception of the double cream, mix all the ingredients together in a saucepan.
2. Stir over a low heat until the mixture comes to the boil, then cook slowly for 20 minutes, stirring occasionally. Remove from the heat and allow to cool.
3. Add the cream and beat until smooth.

DESSERT

CLOOTIE DUMPLING (to feed six)

6 oz self-raising flour
3 oz shredded suet
3 oz demerara sugar
1 apple, peeled and finely
 chopped
3 oz sultanas

2 oz currants
1 egg
1 tablespoon mixed spice
1 tablespoon treacle
¼ pint sour milk

METHOD

1. Mix the ingredients in a bowl in the order given. Warm the milk and dissolve the treacle in it before adding to the mixture to produce a stiff, well-mixed batter. If you stick the mixing spoon in, it should stand upright.
2. Prepare a large pot one third filled with boiling water, put a plate in the bottom, and soak a cotton or linen cloth sufficient in size to hold the batter with the edges gathered up and tied with string.
3. Wring out the boiling cloth, and spread it on your work top.
4. Cover the cloth with a sprinkling of flour and brush evenly over the surface with a pastry brush.
5. Empty the mixture on to the cloth, gather up the edges and tie with a piece of string leaving a little space for the dumpling to swell.
6. Hold the mixture up by the string and smack it all around. This is an important part of the procedure as it adheres the dry flour on the cloth to the batter, which forms a skin round the mixture when it is plunged into the boiling water.
7. Plunge the bag into the boiling water to sit on the plate. The water level should be 2 inches below the string.
8. Boil for 2½ hours, keeping a kettle of water on the boil ready to top up to the desired level.
9. Remove the dumpling from the pot, drain, untie, peel

back the cloth, and turn upside down on to a serving plate.
10. Place the plate in a low oven for 10 minutes until the dumpling has dried and formed a skin.
11. Serve with milk, cream or custard.

P.S.—Leftovers can be fried in butter the next day and served with a sprinkling of castor sugar.

Mrs Wallace, Stromness

RHUBARB DUMPLING

8 oz flour
4 oz margarine
½ teaspoon baking soda
½ teaspoon cream of tartar
2 tablespoons castor sugar

Pinch salt
Milk to mix
Rhubarb
Sugar

METHOD

1. Sieve the flour, sugar, baking soda, cream of tartar and salt.
2. Rub in margarine and make into a paste with milk.
3. Line a greased bowl with the paste.
4. Add some cut rhubarb and sugar.
5. Add another layer of paste, then rhubarb, ending with a layer of paste on top.
6. Cover and steam for 3 hours.

M. Miller, Stronsay

QUICK DUMPLING

1 jar mincemeat
3 oz self-raising flour

1 egg

METHOD

1. Mix mincemeat, flour and egg in a bowl.
2. Put mixture into a well-greased bowl and boil for 2 hours.

E. Shearer, Finstown

78

PINEAPPLE PUDDING

1 cup pineapple juice
1 cup pineapple cubes
1 cup water
Juice of 1 lemon

2 tablespoons cornflour
2 eggs, separated
Whipped cream
½ cup sugar

METHOD

1. Mix the sugar and cornflour together, place them in the top of a double boiler, stir in the pineapple juice, water and lemon juice and cook until smooth.
2. Pour this mixture on to the beaten yolks, fold in the beaten whites, and then add the pineapple cubes.
3. Pour into a buttered baking dish and bake in oven for 20 minutes (325°), (mark 3).
4. When cool, top with whipped cream to serve.

L. Flett, Orphir

BREAD PUDDING

½ lb scraps of bread
1 tablespoon sugar
1 tablespoon suet
1 teacup currants or raisins

½ teaspoon ground ginger
1 teacup milk
1 egg

METHOD

1. Cut crusts from bread and soak in a basin of water for 1 hour.
2. Squeeze out the water and put bread into a dry basin.
3. Add sugar, suet, and fruit.
4. Boil the milk, pour over the dry ingredients and whisk well with a fork.
5. Beat up the eggs and add with the ginger.
6. Butter a pudding bowl, put in the mixture and steam for 1½ hours.
7. Serve with a sweet sauce.

T. Robertson, Longhope

BREAD AND BUTTER PUDDING

Slices of bread and butter   1½ pints milk
2 oz sugar   ¼ lb sultanas
3 eggs   A grate of nutmeg

METHOD

1. Thickly butter slices of bread and put a layer in the bottom of a pie-dish. Sprinkle on the sultanas and repeat the layers until the dish is full.
2. Boil the milk, and pour it on to the well-beaten eggs. Add the sugar and spice then pour it over the contents of the dish.
3. Bake in oven for 1 hour (325°), (mark 3).

P. Firth, Stromness

GREEN ISLAND SEVEN CUP PUDDING

1 cup flour   1 cup sugar
1 cup breadcrumbs   1 cup milk
1 cup suet   1 teaspoon salt
1 cup raisins   1 teaspoon soda
1 cup currants

METHOD

1. Mix all dry ingredients together.
2. Add the milk and eggs.
3. Put into a bowl, cover and steam for 3 hours.

C. Lyon, Stenness

BANANA FLAN

1 flan case   ½ cup whipped cream
4 bananas   Lemon juice
Redcurrant jelly   ¼ lb black grapes
1 dessertspoon sugar

METHOD

1. Mash the bananas, and mix in the sugar, a squeeze of lemon juice and finally the whipped cream.
2. Spread the base of the flan case with redcurrant jelly, spread on the banana mixture and decorate with halved grapes.

N. Wylie, Kirkwall

GRAEMSAY SPICED APPLE TART

Filling

3 apples   2 oz sugar
¼ lb prunes   ½ teaspoon mixed
         spice

Pastry

8 oz flour   ½ teaspoon salt
4 oz margarine   ½ teaspoon cinnamon
1 egg   Cold water to mix
½ oz sugar

METHOD

1. Stew the apples, prunes, sugar and spices together.
2. Remove the prune stones and let the mixture cool.
3. Make the pastry by rubbing fat into flour, add dry

81

F

ingredients, beaten egg and enough water to make a stiff consistency.

4. Set aside a third of the pastry and roll out the rest to line the bottom of your tin.
5. Add the filling, which must be cold.
6. Roll out the remainder of the pastry and put on the top.
7. Bake in oven for 30-40 minutes (350°), (mark 4).
8. Dust with castor sugar to serve.

C. Lyon, Stennes

APPLE MERINGUE PIE

3 cups hot, sweetened
  stewed apples
½ teaspoon grated lemon rind
2 eggs

2 tablespoons melted butter
2 tablespoons castor sugar
4 oz shortcrust pastry

METHOD

1. Line a pie-plate with short pastry. Prick the crust all over to prevent it from rising, and bake it in the oven for 20 minutes (375°), (mark 5) till crisp and pale golden.
2. Mix the apples with the melted butter, grated lemon rind and the well-beaten egg yolks.
3. Fill this mixture into the pastry shell when it is cold.
4. Beat the whites of the eggs till stiff, beat in two-thirds of the sugar until very stiff, fold in the remainder of the sugar, and pile on top of the pie.
5. Put in oven for 10 minutes (325°), (mark 3) to set.

L. Allan, Stromness

MARMALADE PEARS

1 large can pear halves   6 oz sweet orange marmalade
1 teaspoon butter   Whipped cream

METHOD

1. Heat the pears in a saucepan. When they are hot, lift
   them out and keep them warm in the oven.
2. Measure half a pint of the pear juice into a saucepan
   and cook for 5 minutes. Stir in the marmalade and
   simmer for a few minutes then remove from the heat
   and stir in the butter until melted.
3. Pour marmalade mixture over the pear halves and
   serve at once with whipped cream.

T. Mackay, Stromness

RHUBARB JELLY

1 lb fresh rhubarb $\frac{1}{2}$ lb castor sugar
2$\frac{1}{2}$ oz cornflour

METHOD

1. Cut the rhubarb into pieces, put in a saucepan, add the
   sugar and enough water to cover. Stew for 10 minutes
   until soft.
2. Strain the rhubarb through a cloth. There should be 1$\frac{1}{2}$
   pints of juice. Make up with a little water if short.
3. Mix the cornflour to a smooth cream with a little of the
   juice. Bring the rest of the juice to the boil and pour it
   into the mixed cornflour, stirring all the time.
4. Return it to the saucepan, and boil for 3 minutes.
5. Pour into a mould and allow to cool. When cold, turn
   it out and serve with custard or cream.

T. Eunson, Kirkwall

APPLE AND MINCEMEAT SPONGE

½ lb cooking apples   1 oz margarine
2 dessertspoons sweet   3 oz sugar
    mincemeat   2½ oz self-raising flour
1 egg   Milk to mix

METHOD

1. Peel and cut apples and place in a pan with 1½ cups
   of water and 1 oz of sugar.
2. Simmer until tender.
3. Grease a pie dish and put in the stewed apples.
4. Spread the mincemeat over the apples.
5. Beat the margarine and sugar together.
6. Add the egg and flour and beat well. If necessary, add a
   little milk to make a thick creamy consistency.
7. Pour the mixture over the apples and mincemeat.
8. Bake for 30-40 minutes in oven (375°), (mark 5).

J. Wilkie, Evie

BANANA CHARLOTTE

8 ripe bananas   2 oz castor sugar
4 dessertspoons apricot jam   ¼ lb fresh butter
1 lemon   Wineglass of rum
Slices of bread

METHOD

1. Thickly butter a deep pie-dish.
2. Cut a thin piece of bread to cover the bottom of the
   dish, butter both sides and fit it in.
3. Cut oblong slices of bread, butter on both sides, and
   line the sides of the mould overlapping slightly.
4. Cut the bananas in half lengthways and then quarter

lengthways. Place the pieces in a dish and pour on the glass of rum and the juice of the lemon and let them soak for some time. Sprinkle with sugar.

5. Place a layer of the bananas into the mould and spread a layer of apricot jam on top. Repeat the process until the mould is full.
6. Pour the rum over the bananas in the mould and cover with more slices of buttered bread.
7. Bake in oven for 1 hour (350°), (mark 4) until brown.
8. Turn out on to a hot dish and serve with custard or cream.

S. Croy, Kirkwall

TRIFLE

1 pint cream	Strawberry jam
1 pint custard	$\frac{1}{2}$ pint sherry
6 stale sponge cakes	$\frac{1}{4}$ pint brandy
12 macaroons	$\frac{1}{4}$ pint water
$\frac{1}{4}$ lb ratafias	

METHOD

1. Mix the sherry, brandy and water together.
2. Spread a layer of jam on the bottom of the bowl.
3. Cut the cakes in half, dip them into the wine and water, and put a layer on the jam.
4. Dip some macaroons and ratafias in the wine, and put them on the layer of sponge cake.
5. Pour on some of the custard, followed by another layer of jam, soaked cakes and the rest of the custard.
6. Whip the cream and spread on the top.

P. Firth, Stromness

GOOSEBERRY FOOL

2 quarts gooseberries   ½ pint thick custard
4 oz sugar   Water
½ pint cream

METHOD

1. Wash the green gooseberries and put them on to boil in half a pint of water. When they turn yellow and are quite soft, turn them out into a coarse sieve over a bowl and press the pulp through the sieve.
2. Stir in ¼ lb of moist sugar and allow it to cool.
3. When cold, add the custard and cream, and mix thoroughly.
4. Serve in a glass dish, or in melba glasses.

N. Drever, Kirkwall

PENTLAND FOAM

6 oz sugar   1½ oz flour
1 oz butter   1 lemon
2 eggs   6 oz milk

METHOD

1. Mix sugar, butter, egg yolks and flour together.
2. Add the grated rind of the lemon, the juice of the lemon and the milk.
3. Fold in the egg whites, stiffly beaten.
4. Place in a buttered dish.
5. Set the dish in a tin of hot water.
6. Bake for 40 minutes in oven (325°), (mark 3).
7. Serve immediately.

J. Flett, Orphir

SURPRISE CHOCOLATE CREAM

½ an orange jelly
½ a packet of marshmallows
1 egg, separated

¼ pint milk
2 tablespoons drinking
    chocolate

METHOD

1. Dissolve the jelly in 4 tablespoons hot water.
2. Stir in the chocolate, and the egg yolk beaten with the milk.
3. Snip the marshmallows into pieces using wet scissors.
4. Fold the stiffly beaten egg whites into the mixture.
5. Put into dish, or dishes, and leave in a cool place to set.

H. Garson, Sandwick

COFFEE SPONGE

1 tablespoon gelatine
1 egg white
2 tablespoons cold water
Salt

½ cup castor sugar
3 cups strong, hot coffee
½ teaspoon vanilla essence

METHOD

1. Cover the gelatine with the cold water, and set aside for 10 minutes.
2. Add the sugar and pour on the hot coffee, stirring until the gelatine is dissolved.
3. Let the mixture cool, add the vanilla essence, and when it is about to set, add the egg white beaten to a stiff froth. Beat until spongy and light.
4. Turn into a mould to set, and serve with vanilla or lemon custard.

N. Eunson, Deerness

STRAWBERRY WHIP

1 cup chopped strawberries   ¼ cup castor sugar
1 dessertspoon sweet sherry   ¼ pint cream
2 egg whites   4 whole strawberries
Pinch salt

METHOD

1. Chop the strawberries in the morning, add the sherry, then keep in the refrigerator until ready to make the whip.
2. Beat the egg whites with the salt until stiff, then beat in sugar gradually until meringue is stiff and glossy.
3. Whip the cream and fold into the meringue, then lastly fold in the strawberries.
4. Divide into 4 dessert dishes and top with a whole strawberry to serve.

J. MacLeod, Kirkwall

WHISKY PEARS

1 lb tin pear halves   Grated walnut
2 tablespoons Highland Park   Chocolate sauce
Vanilla ice cream

METHOD

1. Strain the juice off the pears and mix in the whisky.
2. Mix the grated walnut into the ice cream.
3. Put two scoops of ice cream on to each plate either side of a pear half and top with chocolate sauce.
4. Pour on the whisky juice before serving.

J. Dell, Kirkwall

BAKING

FRUIT CAKE

1 lb self-raising flour	1 lb raisins
½ lb margarine	½ lb glace cherries
½ lb castor sugar	½ pint boiling milk
1 lb sultanas	2 eggs, beaten

METHOD

1. Rub the margarine into the flour.
2. Add sugar and fruit.
3. Pour on the boiling milk and mix well.
4. Add the beaten eggs and mix well.
5. Line a 7-inch cake tin and pour in the mixture.
6. Bake for 2 hours in oven (300°), (mark 2) then reduce the heat to (250°), (mark 1) for a further 2 hours or until firm.
7. Remove cake from the oven and leave for 10 minutes before turning out onto a cooling rack.
8. This cake is best if kept for 1 month in an airtight tin.

J. Wilkie, Evie

FRUIT SLICES

1 lb plain flour	1 egg
½ lb margarine	Pinch of salt
2 teaspoons baking powder	Milk to mix

Filling

1 lb currants	1 dessertspoon mixed spice
¼ lb sugar	Cornflour

METHOD

1. Put the currants, sugar and mixed spice into a pan with a little water and cook for 5 minutes.

2. Add as much cornflour as required to make a thick spreading consistency and leave to cool.
3. Rub the margarine into the flour.
4. Add the salt and half of the beaten egg and enough milk to make a stiff dough.
5. Roll out thinly and use half to line the bottom of a Swiss roll tin.
6. Spread the filling on top of this and cover with the rest of the pastry.
7. Brush with the rest of the egg and prick with a fork.
8. Bake for 25 minutes in oven (375°), (mark 5).

F. Manson, Dounby

FRUIT LOAF

4 oz margarine	1 cup of water
4 oz castor sugar	2 eggs
8 oz self-raising flour	1 teaspoon mixed spice
8 oz mixed dried fruit	1 teaspoon baking soda

METHOD

1. Put margarine, sugar, fruit, spice and soda into a pan with the water.
2. Simmer this mixture for 5 minutes and leave until cold.
3. Add flour and beaten eggs and mix well.
4. Put into a greased loaf tin and bake for 50 minutes in oven (350°), (mark 4).

W. Cursiter, Papa Westray

MALT LOAF

12 oz self-raising flour
¼ teaspoon cream of tartar
¼ teaspoon baking soda
2 tablespoons malt extract

1 oz margarine
2 eggs
2 tablespoons syrup

METHOD

1. Mix all the dry ingredients together and rub in the margarine.
2. Melt the syrup and malt with two tablespoons of milk.
3. Beat the eggs and pour with the syrup mixture on to the dry ingredients.
4. Stir well, and if necessary, add a little milk to make a soft consistency.
5. Pour into a greased loaf tin and bake for 1-1½ hours in oven (350°), (mark 4).

R. Wallace, Shapinsay

GRANDMA'S GINGERBREAD

10 oz plain flour
3 oz butter or margarine
1 cup of milk
4 oz castor sugar
4 oz treacle

2 eggs
1 teaspoon mixed spice
1 teaspoon ginger
1 teaspoon baking soda
Pinch of salt

METHOD

1. Sift the dry ingredients together.
2. Melt the fat with the treacle and add to the mixture with the beaten eggs.
3. Mix to a light batter with the milk and pour into a loaf tin.
4. Bake for 40 minutes in oven (350°), (mark 4).

Mrs Groat, Orphir

BROONIE

6 oz oatmeal
6 oz flour
4 oz butter or margarine
2 oz sugar
2 tablespoons syrup or treacle

1 teaspoon ginger
¾ teaspoon baking soda
Pinch salt
1 egg
Buttermilk to mix

METHOD

1. Mix meal and flour and rub in fat.
2. Add salt, ginger and soda.
3. Melt the treacle and add together with the beaten egg and sufficient buttermilk to let the mixture drop easily from the spoon.
4. Mix thoroughly and put into a greased tin.
5. Bake for 75 minutes in oven (325°), (mark 3) or until well risen and firm in the centre.

B. Leslie, Westray

SANDAY BUN

4 oz plain flour
4 oz self-raising flour
4 oz margarine
4 oz sugar
1 teaspoon baking soda

1 teaspoon cinnamon
1 lb mixed fruit
2 eggs
1 oz mixed peel
1 cup of water

METHOD

1. Put water, sugar, margarine, fruit and soda in a pan and bring slowly to the boil. Boil for 10 minutes.
2. Remove from heat and cool.
3. Add well-beaten eggs, flour and cinnamon and beat well to remove any lumps.
4. Put into a greased loaf tin and bake for 60 minutes in oven (350°), (mark 4).

M. Tulloch, Sanday

CHOCOLATE CAKE WITH DATE FILLING

3 eggs
1 cup sugar
5 tablespoons milk
1½ oz butter

1 cup plain flour
1 tablespoon cocoa
1 teaspoon baking powder

METHOD

1. Beat the eggs and sugar till light and creamy.
2. Put the milk and butter into a pan and bring to the boil.
3. Add the sugar and eggs, flour, baking powder and cocoa.
4. Place in a greased sandwich tin and bake for 20 minutes in oven (350°), (mark 4).

Date Filling

1. Soak 8 dates in hot water with a pinch of soda.
2. Pour off the water and add 1 oz butter and 1 tablespoon of sugar to the dates.
3. Beat until creamy and fill the cake.
4. Ice with chocolate icing.

J. Muir, Stenness

TREACLE SCONES

8 oz plain flour
1 level teaspoon baking soda
1 heaped teaspoon cream
  of tartar
¼ teaspoon cinnamon

¼ teaspoon ginger
½ teaspoon mixed spice
1 tablespoon treacle
Pinch of salt
Milk to mix

METHOD

1. Sieve all the dry ingredients together.
2. Add the treacle on a warm spoon with enough milk to form a soft dough.
3. Shape the mixture as required and bake on a hot girdle browning both sides.

T. Muir, Orphir

GINGER DELIGHT

2 oz butter
½ cup sugar
1 egg, beaten
½ cup golden syrup
½ cup milk
1½ cups flour
1 teaspoon ginger
1 teaspoon cinnamon
1 teaspoon baking soda

METHOD

1. Cream butter and sugar.
2. Add egg, syrup, flour, ginger, cinnamon and soda, and beat well.
3. Add milk and beat again.
4. Divide the mixture into two sandwich tins and bake for 20-25 minutes in oven (350°), (mark 4).

H. Garson, Sandwick

FATTY PANCAKES

8 oz flour
½ teaspoon baking soda
½ teaspoon cream of tartar
Pinch salt
2 tablespoons sugar
2 eggs
6 oz sultanas or quartered cherries
Milk to mix

METHOD

1. Beat the eggs with the sugar.
2. Mix all the dry ingredients together and add the egg mix with sufficient milk to make a consistency suitable for dropped scones.
3. Mix in the sultanas or cherries.
4. Melt sufficient butter in a frying pan to a depth of $\frac{1}{4}''$ and heat till smoking.
5. Drop desertspoonfuls of batter into the fat and cook quickly on both sides.
6. When both sides are golden brown lift on to a cooling rack and sprinkle with sugar.

J. MacLeod, Stromness

ORKNEY OATMEAL SCONES

1 cup plain flour
½ teaspoon baking soda
½ teaspoon cream of
  tartar
1 dessertspoon syrup

1 dessertspoon sugar
1 egg
2 tablespoons porage
  oats

METHOD

1. Mix all ingredients in a bowl adding water to make a thin consistency.
2. Bake 2 tablespoonfuls at a time spread thinly on a hot girdle.

G. Duncan, South Ronaldsay

CLESTRAIN WHEATMEAL SCONES

8 oz wheatmeal flour
6 oz plain flour
1 teaspoon baking soda
1½ teaspoons cream of tartar
Pinch salt
Milk to mix

3 oz margarine
2 oz sultanas
1 tablespoon treacle
1 tablespoon malt extract
1 egg

METHOD

1. Sift all dry ingredients into a bowl of wheatmeal flour.
2. Rub in margarine and add sultanas.
3. Beat malt, treacle, egg and a little milk together and add to dry ingredients.
4. Roll out and cut into shapes.
5. Bake for 15 minutes in oven (425°), (mark 7).

J. Muir, Orphir

POTATO SCONES

½ lb cold boiled potatoes   2 oz flour
½ oz butter   Salt

METHOD

1. Mash the potatoes.
2. Melt the butter and mix with potatoes and salt.
3. Work in as much flour as the paste will take.
4. Roll out very thinly, cut into triangles and place on a hot girdle, pricking well with a fork.
5. Cook for 3 minutes on each side.
6. Can be served hot or cold.

B. Sutherland, Longhope

CREAM SCONES

½ lb flour   1 egg, beaten
1 teaspoon baking powder   ¼ cup sour cream
1 oz butter   Pinch of salt

METHOD

1. Mix the flour, baking powder and salt in a bowl and rub in the butter.
2. Stir in the egg and sour cream to make a moderately soft dough.
3. Turn out on to a floured board and roll out lightly to half an inch in thickness. Prick all over with a fork, cut into rounds and bake on a girdle or in the oven.

N. Bruce, Kirkwall

Pouring a tray of Orkney Fudge at Robertson's confectionery factory in Stromness.

Barrels of Highland Park whisky maturing at the company's warehouse in Kirkwall.

ORCADIAN BERE BANNOCKS

½ lb flour
½ lb beremeal
1 teaspoon baking soda

¼ teaspoon salt
Buttermilk

METHOD

1. Mix all the dry ingredients in a bowl.
2. Add enough buttermilk to make a soft consistency.
3. Shape the bannocks on a board with beremeal.
4. Bake on a hot girdle till lightly browned.
5. Put bannocks on a wire rack and cover with cloth while still hot.

T. Robertson, Longhope

KRAWEN QUARTERS

1 lb plain flour
1 teaspoon baking soda
1 heaped teaspoon cream of tartar
3 oz margarine

1 tablespoon syrup
1½ tablespoons treacle
Pinch of salt
Buttermilk

METHOD

1. Sift the dry ingredients into a bowl and rub in the margarine.
2. Stir in the syrup and treacle and enough buttermilk to make a stiff dough.
3. Roll out onto a floured board and cut into shapes.
4. Bake for 15-20 minutes in oven (475°), (mark 9).

B. Drever, Sanday

PAPIE OATIES

4 oz plain flour
2 level teaspoons baking
   powder
½ teaspoon salt
4 oz rolled oats

2 oz castor sugar
3 oz treacle
4 oz butter or margarine
Coarse oatmeal for
   decoration

METHOD

1. Sift the flour, baking powder and salt together, then add the rolled oats.
2. Put the sugar, treacle and butter into a saucepan and heat until just melted.
3. Cool the mixture slightly, then mix into the flour to form a dough.
4. Sprinkle the surface of the dough with the coarse oatmeal.
5. Press into a greased 7-inch sandwich tin and bake for 20-25 minutes in oven (375°), (mark 5).
6. Cut into wedges before it is cool.
7. Serve with butter and jam or cheese.

E. Davidson, Papa Westray

GRINDLAY MUFFINS

3 cups flour
1 cup sugar
2 oz butter
1 teaspoon baking soda

2 teaspoons cream of tartar
Pinch of salt
Milk to mix

METHOD

1. Sift flour, baking soda and cream of tartar into a bowl.
2. Rub in butter.
3. Add sugar.
4. Add milk to make a soft consistency.
5. Roll out on a floured board to ¼ inch thick.
6. Cut into small rounds and bake on a pre-heated girdle, browning on both sides.

A. Findlay, Stromness

FATTY CUTTIES

3 cups plain flour
3 tablespoons sugar
4 oz currants

8 oz margarine
Pinch of baking soda
Pinch of salt

METHOD

1. Melt the margarine.
2. Mix the dry ingredients together and add the margarine to form a fairly stiff dough.
3. Roll out on a lightly floured board, shape as required and bake on a hot girdle.

L. Mathers, Stenness

ORKNEY PANCAKES

2 teacups oatmeal
Small quantity of sour milk
½ teacup flour
2 teaspoons syrup

1 teaspoon baking soda
1 egg
Milk if necessary

METHOD

1. Soak oatmeal in a little sour milk for 24 hours.
2. Add the flour, baking soda, syrup and the egg.
3. Beat up, adding milk if necessary, to make a fairly thin consistency.
4. Bake on a hot girdle, browning on both sides.
5. Serve with syrup.

E. Thomson, Longhope

101

PANCAKES

2 cups flour
1 level teaspoon baking
  soda
1 level teaspoon cream of
  tartar
1 tablespoon sugar

1 dessertspoon syrup
1 egg
1 oz margarine
Milk to mix
½ level teaspoon salt

METHOD

1. Melt margarine and syrup.
2. Add to dry ingredients and mix.
3. Add beaten egg and enough milk to make a soft dropping
   consistency.
4. Bake on a hot girdle browning on both sides.

M Groat, Longhope

TWATT CINNAMON BUNS

6 oz self-raising flour
3 oz margarine
3 oz sugar
3 oz chopped dates

1 dessertspoon marmalade
1 teaspoon cinnamon
1 beaten egg

METHOD

1. Rub the margarine into the flour.
2. Add the sugar, cinnamon, chopped dates, marmalade
   and the beaten egg.
3. Stir well and form into buns.
4. Bake on a greased tray in oven for 15 minutes (375°),
   (mark 5).

J. Isbister, Twatt

WESTRAY SPICE BUNS

4 oz butter
4 oz sugar
6 oz plain flour
1 large teaspoon ginger
½ teaspoon mixed spice

1 tablespoon treacle
1 tablespoon sweet milk
½ teaspoon baking powder
2 eggs

METHOD

1. Cream the butter and sugar together.
2. Add the dry ingredients, then the milk, treacle and beaten eggs.
3. Mix into a soft consistency and spoon into bun tins.
4. Bake for 20-25 minutes in oven (350°), (mark 4).

L. Mathers, Stenness

CARAMELITAS

5 oz margarine
6 oz plain flour
4 oz crushed oats
¼ teaspoon baking powder
4 oz brown sugar

¼ teaspoon salt
4 tablespoons golden syrup
6 oz plain chocolate
4 oz chopped walnuts

METHOD

1. Melt 3 oz of the margarine in a pan and stir in 4 oz of the flour with the oats, baking powder, sugar and salt.
2. Blend well, and press the mixture into the base of a well greased 9-inch square tin.
3. Bake for 10 minutes in oven (350°), (mark 4).
4. Melt the remaining margarine with the syrup and chocolate.
5. Stir in the remaining flour and add the walnuts.
6. Pour the mixture over the biscuit base and continue to cook for 20-25 minutes.

M. Butcher, South Ronaldsay

SHORTBREAD

4 oz flour	4 oz butter
4 oz rice flour	½ a beaten egg
4 oz castor sugar	2 tablespoons cream

METHOD

1. Sieve the flour and rice flour into a basin, and rub in the butter.
2. Mix in the sugar and bind with the egg and cream.
3. Roll out thinly, cut into fingers and prick with a fork.
3. Bake in oven for 16 minutes (325°), (mark 3) until brown.
4. Cool on a wire rack.

N. Kirk, Kirkwall

CRUNCHY BISCUITS

12 oz plain flour	6 oz demerara sugar
10 oz margarine	Pinch of salt
12 oz soft brown sugar	

METHOD

1. Cream margarine and sugar together.
2. Add the flour and salt to form a dough.
3. Knead lightly, then shape into two rolls approximately 8 inches long.
4. Sprinkle sugar on greaseproof paper, roll the dough in the sugar and wrap it in a clean sheet of greaseproof paper.
5. Place in a refrigerator for about 30 minutes.
6. Cut into ¼ inch slices and bake for 12-15 minutes in oven (325°), (mark 3).

M. Butcher, South Ronaldsay

MANSE BISCUITS

3½ oz self-raising flour
3 oz rolled oats
6 oz demerara sugar

6 oz margarine
¼ teaspoon baking soda
1 dessertspoon water

METHOD

1. Mix the flour, rolled oats and sugar together.
2. Melt the margarine over a low heat and mix into the dry ingredients.
3. Dissolve the baking soda in water and add to the mixture.
4. Blend well, cover, and leave in a cool place for 4-6 hours.
5. Knead the mixture into a dough, roll out and cut into circles.
6. Bake for 12-15 minutes in oven (300°), (mark 2) till brown.

L. Tomison, South Ronaldsay

ROUSAY SHORTBREAD

¾ lb plain flour
¼ lb cornflour

½ lb butter
¼ lb castor sugar

METHOD

1. Mix all the ingredients together and knead into a dough on a cool surface.
2. Roll out to ¼ inch thick, cut into fingers and bake for 40-45 minutes in oven (275°), (mark 1) until golden brown.

Oakleigh Hotel, Stromness

BIRSAY BISCUITS

12 oz self-raising flour
4 oz bere (or bran)
8 oz castor sugar
8 oz margarine

1 egg
6 oz sultanas
A good pinch of salt

METHOD

1. Cream sugar and margarine.
2. Sieve in flour, add bere, sultanas, egg and salt, and mix well.
3. Turn out on to a floured board, knead into a dough, roll out and cut into large biscuit shapes.
4. Grease a tray and bake the biscuits on the top shelf for 16 minutes (350°), (mark 4).
5. Transfer from the baking tray to the cooling rack with a fish lifter, as the biscuits will still be soft, but will become crisp as they cool.

J. Scott, Birsay

CARAMEL SQUARES

6 oz flour
4 oz margarine
1 teaspoon syrup
1 teaspoon baking powder
3 oz brown sugar

5 oz mixed fruit
1 oz chopped nuts
1 egg
Pinch salt
½ teaspoon vanilla essence

Icing

1 large cup of sugar
½ cup creamy milk

1 tablespoon butter

METHOD

1. Melt the margarine with the sugar and syrup and beat well.
2. When cool, beat again, and add dry ingredients, vanilla, and finally the beaten egg.

3. Put in a shallow greased baking tin and bake for 30 minutes in oven (350°), (mark 4).
4. Leave the cake to cool.
5. Prepare the icing by boiling the sugar, milk and butter together, stirring the mixture until it thickens, and spread over the cake while the icing is still warm.
6. Cut into squares.

L. Mathers, Stenness

UNBAKED BUTTERSCOTCH COOKIES

8 oz sugar
6 oz butter or margarine
3 oz can evaporated milk

5 oz rolled oats
½ packet of instant butter-
scotch or caramel whip

METHOD

1. Put the sugar, butter and evaporated milk into a large pan and bring gently to the boil.
2. Remove from the heat and add the instant whip and rolled oats.
3. Beat thoroughly together.
4. Leave to cool for 15 minutes.
5. Drop teaspoonfuls on to a greaseproof paper lined tray and leave to set.

H. Garson, Sandwick

CRUNCHY FLAPJACKS

3 oz margarine
1 tablespoon syrup

1 level tablespoon castor sugar
7 oz Kelloggs country store

METHOD

1. Melt butter, syrup and sugar gently in a pan.
2. Remove from heat and mix in country store.
3. Press into a greased 7″ tin and bake for 20-25 minutes in oven (350°), (mark 4).
4. Leave in tin to cool, then cut into bars.

M. Leslie, Sanday

RICE BISCUITS

2 egg yolks
2 egg whites
1½ oz castor sugar
1½ oz flour

1 teaspoon ground rice
Pinch of cream of tartar
Pinch of baking soda

METHOD

1. Beat the egg yolks and sugar until thick.
2. Add the egg whites and beat again until very thick.
3. Add the dry ingredients and mix well.
4. Drop spoonfuls on to a greased tray.
5. Bake in oven for 12 minutes (325°), (mark 3).
6. Cool on a wire rack.

S. Laird, Kirkwall

CHOCOLATE CRUNCHIES

4 oz plain chocolate   1 egg, beaten
4 oz crushed sweet biscuits   2 oz raisins
Knob of butter   12 paper cake cases

METHOD

1. Melt the chocolate in a bowl over hot water.
2. Crush the biscuits.
3. Add the butter to the melted chocolate. Take off the heat and add the biscuit crumbs, egg and raisins. Mix well.
4. Put a dessertspoonful of the mixture into each case and allow to set.

J. Dell, Kirkwall

CINNAMON BISCUITS

3½ oz flour   2 oz butter
½ teaspoon ground cinnamon   ½ egg
¼ teaspoon baking powder   Milk if required
2 oz sugar   Jam

METHOD

1. Mix the dry ingredients together; rub in the butter, add the half egg and mix to a firm paste.
2. Roll out thinly and cut into rounds.
3. Bake for 15 minutes in oven (300°), (mark 2).
4. Allow to cool, then sandwich two together with jam.

B. Peace, Kirkwall

LEMON BISCUITS

8 oz flour	1 egg yolk
4 oz butter	Rind of 1 lemon, grated
4 oz sugar	

METHOD

1. Cream the butter with the sugar, add the lemon rind and egg yolk and beat well.
2. Mix in the flour to make a soft, light dough.
3. Roll out thinly and cut into rounds.
4. Bake in oven (325°), (mark 3) until golden brown.

J. Scott, Birsay

CRUNCHY PEANUT COOKIES

2 oz soft butter	1 teaspoon vanilla
2 oz crunchy peanut butter	essence
3 oz soft brown sugar	5 oz self-raising flour

METHOD

1. Heat oven (350°), (mark 4).
2. Cream the butter, peanut butter, sugar and vanilla essence together until light and fluffy then stir in the flour with a fork.
3. Divide into 30 equal amounts and transfer to a greased baking tray spaced to allow spread.
4. Flatten the portions with a fork then bake in oven for 12 minutes.

J. Watt, Kirkwall

PRESERVES

BEETROOT CHUTNEY

2 lb cooked beetroot
2 lb peeled and cored apples
1 lb onions
½ lb raisins
½ lb sultanas

½ lb sugar
2 teaspoons ground ginger
2 teaspoons cinnamon
1 pint vinegar
Salt

METHOD

1. Dice the beetroot into a large basin.
2. Finely chop the apples and onion and cook gently in the vinegar.
3. Add the fruit, spices, sugar and salt and simmer gently for 15 minutes.
4. When the mixture has cooled, mix carefully with the beetroot in the basin.
5. Spoon into prepared jars and cover tightly.

H. Garson, Sandwick

WESTFIELD CHUTNEY

1 lb tomatoes
1 lb onions
1 lb apples
1 lb prunes

2 lb brown sugar
1 pint vinegar
2 teaspoons dry mustard
Salt

METHOD

1. Skin and chop tomatoes, onions, apples and stone and chop the prunes.
2. Put all the ingredients except the vinegar into a pan and heat slowly until the sugar is dissolved then simmer for a further 30 minutes.
3. Add the vinegar and cook for another 30 minutes.
4. Pour into prepared jars, allow to cool, then cover tightly.

M. Lyon, Stromness

RHUBARB AND ORANGE CHUTNEY

1 pint vinegar	1 teaspoon ground ginger
2 lb brown sugar	½ level teaspoon mixed spice
2 lb rhubarb	2 tablespoons undiluted
1 lb onions	orange squash
¾ lb sultanas	Salt

METHOD

1. Cut the rhubarb into small pieces and chop the onion.
2. Put all the ingredients into a pan.
3. Heat gently and simmer for 45-50 minutes or until the mixture thickens.
4. Pour into prepared jars, allow to cool, then cover tightly.

M. Flett, Birsay

CAULIFLOWER CHUTNEY

2 large cauliflower	1 teaspoon all spice
1 lb onions	2 teaspoons dry mustard
¾ pint vinegar	2 heaped teaspoons tumeric
½ lb sugar	Salt
2 heaped teaspoons curry powder	

METHOD

1. Break the cauliflower into small pieces and chop the onion finely.
2. Put both these ingredients into a bowl, sprinkle with salt and leave to stand overnight.
3. Bring the vinegar to the boil then add the sugar, cauliflower and the spices.
4. Boil for 30 minutes, then, if required, thicken with a little cornflour mixed in cold vinegar.
5. Spoon into prepared jars, allow to cool, then cover tightly.

B. Coghill, Birsay

GOOSEBERRY CHUTNEY

2 lb green gooseberries
¼ lb onions
¼ lb sultanas
1 lb demerara sugar

1 teaspoon cayenne pepper
2 teaspoons ground ginger
2 teaspoons salt
1 pint malt vinegar

METHOD

1. Top and tail the gooseberries and chop up the onion.
2. Put all the ingredients in a pan and simmer gently for 1½ hours or until the gooseberry skins are tender.
3. Pour into prepared jars, allow to cool, then cover tightly.
4. This chutney improves if kept for a while.

E. Williams, Orphir

POMONA PICKLE

1 lb stoned dates, finely chopped
1 lb onions, finely chopped
1 lb cooking apples, grated
1 lb demerara sugar

1 teaspoon dry English mustard
½ teaspoon salt
½ teaspoon pepper
1 pint malt vinegar

METHOD

1. Mix the dry ingredients together in a bowl.
2. Mix in the malt vinegar.
3. Leave uncovered overnight.
4. Pour into jars and seal tightly.

L. Whitie, Kirkwall

RHUBARB JAM WITH CLOVES

7 lb rhubarb   A few cloves
7 lb sugar

METHOD

1. Cut the rhubarb into 1-inch pieces, cover with the sugar, and stand overnight.
2. Tie the cloves in a muslin bag and place in a jelly-pan with the rhubarb and sugar and boil for 1½ hours. Remove the bag of cloves and test the jam to set.
3. Pour into prepared jars to cool, then cover tightly.

Oakleigh Hotel, Stromness

APRICOT JAM

1 lb dried apricots   3½ pints boiling water
4 lb sugar

METHOD

1. Wash and quarter the apricots.
2. Pour the boiling water over them and stand for 24 hours.
3. Boil in a pan for 1 hour, add the sugar, and boil for another 30 minutes.
4. Pour into prepared jars and cover tightly.

H. Garson, Sandwick

BANANA JAM

12 large bananas (not too ripe)
6 sweet oranges

4 lemons
¾ lb sugar for every pound of bananas

METHOD

1. Peel the bananas and cut them into thin slices.
2. Squeeze the juice from the oranges and lemons.
3. Put the bananas, fruit juice and sugar into a large pan.
4. Boil slowly for 45 minutes.
5. Skim, test, and when ready, pour into prepared jars and cover tightly.

H. Garson, Sandwick

CHERRY CURRANT JAM

2 lb cherries
1½ lb red currants

2½ lb sugar
1 cup water

METHOD

1. Wash the currants and put them in a pan with the water and heat gently, mashing them with a wooden spoon.
2. Simmer for 10 minutes or till all juice is extracted, then strain through a jelly-bag obtaining as much juice as possible.
3. Put the juice in a pan with the stoned cherries and simmer for 10 minutes.
4. Add the sugar and stir till dissolved and boiling.
5. Boil briskly for 10-15 minutes or till jam sets when tested.

A. Petrie, Stromness

FOUR-FRUIT JELLY

Equal quantities of

Cherries	Strawberries
Red currants	Raspberries

1 lb of sugar to each lb of juice.

METHOD

1. Prepare fruits and put them in a double saucepan and simmer for 1½ hours, crushing and mashing occasionally to extract the juice.
2. When the fruit is quite soft, strain off the juice through a jelly-bag.
3. Measure the quantity of juice and put it in a jelly-pan with the proportionate amount of sugar and stir till dissolved and boiling.
4. Boil briskly for 10-15 minutes till jelly sets when tested.

L. Laughton, Kirkwall

STRAWBERRY AND RHUBARB JAM

3 lb strawberries	3¾ lb sugar
2 lb red rhubarb	1 teaspoon citric acid

METHOD

1. Cut the rhubarb into inch pieces and layer in a basin with the strawberries and sugar overnight.
2. Turn into a jelly-pan, add the citric acid and stir with a wooden spoon over moderate heat until boiling.
3. Boil for 15 minutes then test to set.

L. Laughton, Kirkwall

BLACKCURRANT JAM

2 lb blackcurrants   3½ lb sugar
2 pints water

METHOD

1. Stalk and wash the currants (note that the green bud should not be removed as this improves the flavour and set of the jam).
2. Put the fruit in a pan with the water and boil for 15 minutes keeping up the quantity to at least two-thirds of the original.
3. Add the warmed sugar and stir till boiling. Boil briskly until jam sets when tested (approximately 10 minutes).

S. Laird, Kirkwall

MARMALADE

2lb marmalade oranges   4 pints water
2 lemons   6 lb sugar

METHOD

1. Cut or mince the fruit finely and soak for 24 hours in the water. Keep the pips and centre pith separate in a small bowl covered with water.
2. After soaking the pips, tie them securely in a muslin bag and boil with the fruit for 1½ hours, or until the peel is tender and the liquid reduced by half.
3. Remove the bag of pips.
4. Add the sugar and bring back to the boil.
5. Test for set after 15 minutes.
6. When ready, pour into prepared jars and cover tightly.

B. Wick, Sandwick

LEMON MARMALADE

Lemons   Water
Sugar

METHOD

1. Slice the lemons very thinly and remove the pips.
2. To each pound of sliced fruit add 3 pints of cold water and let it stand for 24 hours.
3. Put the lemon and water into a pan, and boil until the lemon is tender. Pour it all into a large bowl and let it stand until the next day.
4. Measure the lemon and water, and to each pint add 1½ lbs sugar.
5. Boil together until the syrup jellies. Test on a cold plate.

I. Flett, Kirkwall

GRAPEFRUIT MARMALADE

4 grapefruits   4 pints water
4 lemons   Sugar

METHOD

1. Put the 4 grapefruits into a pan with sufficient cold water to cover them. Bring to the boil and cook slowly until they are tender and can be easily pierced with a fork.
2. Remove the pan from the heat and leave it to stand overnight.
3. Cut the lemons in half, squeeze out the juice and strain it into a basin. Add the pips, tied in a piece of muslin, together with the rind of the lemon thinly sliced. Pour on 4 pints of water and leave it to stand overnight.
4. Drain the grapefruit from the water, cut them in half, scoop out the pulp, put it in a strainer and squeeze out all the juice, discarding the pips and the pulp, but retain the rind, which should be thinly sliced and put

118

in the jelly-pan with the juice of the grapefruits and lemons.
5. Boil slowly until the liquid is reduced by half.
6. Measure the fruit, and for each pint allocate 1½lb sugar.
7. Bring the fruit back to the boil, add the sugar, stirring constantly until it has dissolved, then boil slowly until the marmalade will set when tested on a cold saucer.

L. Craigie, Kirkwall

ORANGE MARMALADE

9 Seville oranges	Sugar
2 sweet oranges	Water
2 lemons	

METHOD

1. Cut the fruit across into thin slices. Put the pips aside, cover the fruit with 9 pints of cold water and let it stand for 24 hours.
2. Put the fruit into a jelly pan, add the pips tied in a muslin bag, and boil gently for about 1 hour, or until it has been reduced by half.
3. Strain through a jelly-bag or clean cloth and allow to drip overnight.
4. Measure the juice, and to each pint add 1 lb of sugar.
5. Boil and test on a cold saucer until the marmalade will set.

L. Craigie, Kirkwall

119

APPLE MARMALADE

Cooking apples
Sugar
Cloves

Lemon peel
Water

METHOD

1. Peel, core and thinly slice the apples.
2. Allow ¾ lb of loaf sugar for each lb of prepared apples.
3. Put the sugar into the preserving pan with a little water (half a cup to 6 lb sugar), let the sugar melt, then boil it for 10 minutes.
4. Put in the prepared apple, with a few cloves and a little lemon peel and boil for 1 hour. Stir and skim well.
5. It should now be completely smooth, fairly clear and a bright amber colour. Test on a cold plate to set.

P. Miller, Kirkwall

LEMON CURD

3 oz butter
8 oz sugar
3 eggs

Grated rind of 1 lemon
Juice of two lemons
2 teaspoons cornflour

METHOD

1. Melt the butter gently over a low heat.
2. Add the sugar and rind and heat slowly until the sugar has melted.
3. Add the cornflour with the lemon juice.
4. Remove the pan from the heat, beat the eggs, and stir in slowly.
5. Heat the mixture until it thickens but do not allow to boil.
6. Put into prepared jars, allow to cool, then cover tightly.

H. Garson, Sandwick

CONFECTIONERY

TABLET

4 oz Butter
3 lb sugar
8 oz tin condensed
  milk

1 cup milk
1 cup water
Vanilla essence

METHOD

1. Melt the butter in a saucepan, add sugar, water and plain milk and bring slowly to boil for 5 minutes. Remove from the heat and leave for 5 minutes.
2. Add the condensed milk and, stirring occasionally, cook slowly until a little dropped into cold water forms a caramel consistency.
3. Add 1 teaspoon of vanilla essence.
4. Remove from heat, beat thoroughly with a wooden spoon, then pour into a greased tin.
5. Mark into squares when nearly cold.

J. Bain, Westray

TREACLE TOFFEE

¼ lb butter
½ lb treacle

½ lb demerara sugar

METHOD

1. Put the butter into a saucepan, and when partially melted, add the treacle and the sugar. Mix well together, then boil for 8-10 minutes.
2. Test by dropping a little into cold water. If it immediately hardens and is brittle, it is ready to pour out on to a buttered tray.
3. Before it is hard, mark into squares with the back of a knife.

N. Anderson, Kirkwall

121

BUTTERSCOTCH

8 oz demerara sugar   1 cup water
2 oz butter   1 tablespoon vinegar

METHOD

1. Mix all the ingredients in a pan and heat gently until the sugar dissolves.
2. Boil briskly for 5 minutes without stirring until the mixture thickens and turns golden brown.
3. Test a little of the mixture in cold water, if it sets, pour into a greased tin and cut into squares just before it sets.

N. Kirk, Kirkwall

BARLEY SUGAR

1½ lb castor sugar   ½ pint of water
½ white of 1 egg   1 teaspoon lemon juice

METHOD

1. Put the sugar into a saucepan with the water and egg white and mix well.
2. Bring to the boil and skim carefully. As soon as the scum ceases to rise, the sugar is clarified.
3. Boil until a little dropped into cold water becomes hard and brittle.
4. Remove from the heat, mix in the lemon juice, let it stand for a minute, then pour on to an oiled tray. Before it sets hard, cut into strips and twist them.

N. Anderson, Kirkwall

ROYAL FUDGE

1 lb brown sugar   Knob of butter
1 cup walnuts   Grated rind of 1 orange

METHOD

1. Put all the ingredients into a saucepan, stir until the sugar has dissolved and the mixture comes to the boil.
2. Boil for 3 minutes. Remove the pan from the heat and beat the mixture until it thickens.
3. Pour into a buttered tin and cut into squares when cold.

L. Allan, Stromness

PEPPERMINT CREAMS

1½ lb icing sugar   Water
1 egg white   Peppermint essence

METHOD

1. Put the egg white and an equal quantity of water in a bowl with a little peppermint essence and gradually add sufficient icing sugar to make a stiff dough.
2. Roll out the dough to a quarter of an inch in thickness and cut into small rounds. Place on a smooth tray dusted with icing sugar to dry. Ready to eat in 12 hours.

T. Findlay, Stromness

FRUIT CREAM BARS

1½ lb icing sugar   Water
1 egg white   Preserved fruits
                      Assorted fruits

METHOD

1. Put the egg white and an equal quantity of water in a bowl and gradually add sufficient icing sugar to make a stiff dough.
2. Chop up some assorted preserved fruits such as glace cherries, figs, raisins and a little peel. Work this into the sugar cream, then roll out to three quarters of an inch thick.
3. Cut into bars and place to dry on a smooth tray dusted with icing sugar. Ready to eat in 12 hours.

T. Findlay, Stromness

CANDIED ORANGE

1 tin of mandarin oranges   ¼ pint water
½ lb cane sugar

METHOD

1. Strain the juice off the oranges and dry them on kitchen paper.
2. Boil the sugar and the water to the "crack". This is when a little dropped into cold water sets hard and brittle. Remove from the heat.
3. Stick each piece of orange on a skewer and dip it into the syrup. Remove any strands hanging beneath, and lay the oranges on a tray to set.

L. Wallace, Kirkwall

HOME-BREW

HOME-BREWED ALE

The secrets of real Orkney home brewed ale are, I suspect, as lost nowadays as the famous heather ale of the R. L. Stevenson ballad. I have tasted it once or twice in the 1940s — a marvellous unforgettable experience.

In the late twentieth century, nearly everything is second-rate; easily achieved, soon to be discarded. The beauty of craftsmanship — "a joy for ever" — is unknown in these giddy shallow whirling times.

This is not to say that "instant home-brew" is not worth drinking. I know brewers who make excellent ale out of extract of malt and sugar. But it resembles real ale as a cleverly-taken photo resembles an old master.

What to do

Buy a plastic dustbin, capacity 4 gallons or thereby.

Decant into it a 2 lb or 2½ lb tin of hop-flavoured extract of malt. It lies there like dark sweet lava. Over the lava pour a 2 lb (or the nearest European equivalent) poke of sugar; frosted snow, it lies on the lava: impotent as yet.

With a kettle of warm water dissolve the malt extract and the sugar, stirring at first stickily and at last fluently with a wooden spoon.

Add a couple of teaspoons of salt.

With warm water make up the level to within 3 or 4 inches of the top of the bin.

When the sticky rather ugly-looking mixture stands at bloodheat — the same as you and me — sprinkle on the magic ingredient, yeast (you can buy it by the packet, quite cheap).

For a while nothing happens. The grains of yeast swell, coagulate, form a mild mass on the surface of the dark tarn. But a mystery is happening. Lift the lid after a few hours, and a noble saffron head of froth presents itself. Tilt your ear, you can detect a seething, an endless sussuration, the song of Barleycorn. The yeast is slowly transforming the malt sugars and cane sugars into alcohol. It is a work not to be hurried; it

125

takes days for the process to work itself out. In summer the merry battle is over faster than in the cold months.

When the yeast has stopped working, and the surface of the liquor looks (again) like a dark inert tarn, the time has come to empty the brew into clean bottles.

Store the full bottles like precious ingots in the vault of the cupboard. Be patient for at least a fortnight. If you have the strength to feast nothing more than your eyes on it for a month or 5 weeks, all the better.

Then, some cold disagreeable evening, blow up the fire, open a couple of bottles, sip, swallow, and behold the squandering in defeat of many of the miseries of this world.

George Mackay Brown, Stromness

ORKNEY ALE

14 lb malt
2 oz hops
1¼ lb sugar

8 gallon water
1 oz baker's yeast

METHOD

1. See that the vessel is spotlessly clean then put in the malt.
2. Bring the water almost to boiling point and pour it over the malt. Cover lightly, and let it mask for 3 hours.
3. Strain the mixture, and add the hops (tied in a muslin bag to save straining) and 1 lb of sugar. Boil for 1 hour.
4. Return the liquor to the vessel, and when it has cooled to blood heat, add the yeast which may be "started" by sprinkling with a little sugar or by frothing in a little of the warm liquor then diluted before adding to the vessel to start fermentation.
5. When fermentation has ceased (usually after 2 or 3 days), skim the surface, allow to settle, bottle and cork tightly. Half a teaspoon of sugar may be added to each bottle if desired.

F. Marian McNeill

BIRSAY BREW

Heather blossom	Honey or syrup
Ginger	Yeast
Hops	Water

1. Gather a large quantity of fully bloomed heather blossom.
2. Cover with water in a large pot and boil for one hour.
3. Strain and measure the liquid. For every 1½ gallons of liquid add 1 oz ginger, ½ oz hops and 1 lb of honey or syrup.
4. Boil for 20 minutes.
5. Cool to lukewarm, then add ½ oz of brewers yeast for every 1½ gallons of liquid.
6. Cover with a cloth until the next day, then skim, bottle and cork loosely for a few days until fermentation has ceased, then cork tightly.
7. Ready to drink after 2 months, but improves with age.

E. Moar, Dounby

TATTIE WINE

10 medium sized potatoes	2 lb raisins
1 orange	1 oz fresh yeast
2 lemons	10 pints boiling water
6 lb sugar	

METHOD

1. Wash the potatoes, (do not peel) and cut them into small slices.
2. Cut the unpeeled lemons and orange into thin slices.
3. Put these ingredients into a large vessel, add the raisins and sugar and pour on the boiling water.
4. Allow to stand until lukewarm, then add the yeast.
5. Cover and stir daily for 10 days till quite flat.
6. Strain and bottle. Cork loosely for the first 3 weeks then cork tightly.
7. Ready to drink after 6 months.

E. Laird, Harray

RHUBARB WINE

5 lbs rhubarb
3 lbs sugar
2 lemons

1 oz fresh yeast
1 gallon of boiling water

METHOD

1. Chop up rhubarb and lemons and add with the sugar to the boiling water.
2. Allow to cool until lukewarm.
3. Spread the yeast on a piece of toast and let it float in the liquid.
4. Cover with a cloth and let it stand for 3 weeks.
5. Strain off the liquid, bottle and cork.
6. Ready to drink after 6 months.

I. Sinclair, Sandwick

SWEET SHERRY WINE

4 lb brown sugar
2 lb green grapes
1 lb raisins

6 potatoes thinly sliced
1 oz fresh yeast
1 gallon boiling water

METHOD

1. Crush the grapes and add to the boiling water with the potatoes, raisins and sugar.
2. Allow to cool till lukewarm then add the yeast.
3. Cover and stir daily for 3 weeks.
4. Filter and bottle and allow to stand for 3 weeks loosely corked then cork tightly.
5. Ready to drink in 6 weeks.

H. Garson, Sandwick

RURAL LIQUEUR

1 bottle cider
1 bottle rose hip
  syrup

1 cup whisky
6 oz sugar

METHOD

Mix all ingredients together and stir well until the sugar has dissolved. Bottle and keep for 3 weeks before drinking.

R. Wallace, Shapinsay

ATHOLE BROSE

1½ cups double cream
1 cup lightly toasted oatmeal

½ cup heather honey
2 wine glasses Highland Park

METHOD

1. Beat the cream to a froth.
2. Stir in the oatmeal, followed by the honey.
3. Just before the serving, mix in the whisky.

F. Marian McNeill

OATMEAL NOG

1 tablespoon oatmeal
1 tablespoon Highland Park

1 tablespoon honey
½ pint milk
Pinch of salt

METHOD

1. Heat the milk and pour it over the oatmeal in a small bowl. Cover, and leave for 1 hour, then strain, squeezing the meal dry.
2. Return the mealy milk to the pan, add the salt and the honey, bring to the boil and simmer for 10 minutes.
3. Pour into a tumbler, add the whisky, and drink hot.

F. Marian McNeill

129

I

ADVOCAT

3 large eggs
3 lemons
1 lb castor sugar

1 large tin evaporated
milk
¼ pint of brandy

METHOD

1. Break the eggs and shells into a basin and cover with the juice of the lemons.
2. Keep turning the eggs in the juice for three days.
3. Strain the eggs and juice through muslin into a large baking bowl.
4. Add the sugar, milk and brandy and whisk together until frothy.
5. Bottle and drink as soon as you like.

I. Sinclair, Sandwick

CAMERON'S KICK

⅓ Highland Park
⅓ Irish whisky

⅙ lemon juice
⅙ orgeat syrup

Shake well and strain into cocktail glasses.

F. Marian McNeill

DEWAR'S DRINK

⅗ Highland Park
⅖ ginger wine

Named after the late Dr James Dewar of St Margaret's Hope, South Ronaldsay, who, after exposure to high gales and wild seas when visiting patients in his island group, would concoct this drink as a restorative.

F. Marian McNeill

HOUSEHOLD HINTS

APPLES—To peel: Drop a few drops of lemon juice into a pan of cold water. As you pare the apples drop them into the water and they will retain their colour.

BACON—To cook: Hold each slice of bacon under the cold water tap for a few seconds, wipe off the water, then lay the bacon in an earthenware or enamel dish, instead of a frying pan, and cook in a hot oven for a few minutes. This method preserves the fat, and the flavour is improved.

CUSTARD—To stop a skin forming on custard, sprinkle the top with sugar.

DRIED BEANS AND PEAS—To boil: Soak overnight in water with a teaspoonful of sodium bicarbonate added. They will retain their colour and be nice and soft.

BREAD—To keep fresh: Wash and dry a large potato and put it in the bottom of your bread bin.

NEW BREAD—To cut: Dip the bread knife in boiling water and new bread will cut quite easily.

BUTTER—To cream: Butter will cream more easily if placed in a basin which has just been rinsed with boiling water.

CABBAGE—To make digestible: When half-boiled, pour off the water and add fresh boiling water.

CAKE—To keep moist: Keep part of a loaf of bread with your cake in a tin with a close fitting lid, and the cake will not get dry.

CAKE—To remove from tin: Place the baking tin in a basin of hot water for a few seconds. The heat loosens the cake and it can then be easily turned out.

CAKE-MAKING HINT—To prevent the fruit from sinking, dredge a little flour over the raisins, etc., before adding them to the rest of the ingredients.

CHEESE—To prevent it turning dry: Wrap it in a damp muslin cloth and sprinkle with vinegar. Keep in a cool, raised covered dish.

DRIPPING—To clarify: Chop the dripping, and put it into a saucepan with enough water to cover well. Let it boil without a lid until the liquid no longer looks milky, but is oily. Let it cool a little, then strain through a coarse piece of calico into a clean basin.

FISH-BONE—To remove: The juice slowly sucked from half a lemon will often remove a fish bone that has become lodged in the throat.

FISHY SMELL—To remove from saucepan: Empty tea leaves into the pan, cover with water; leave for a few minutes, rinse out and all taste or smell of fish will have gone.

GAME—To test if hung: Pull a feather from the lower part of the back near the tail. If it comes out quite easily, the bird is "high" enough for the average consumer.

GREENS—To boil: Add a piece of fat about the size of your thumb to the water, and it will not boil over.

HAM—An excellent way to boil: Wrap your ham in greaseproof paper and put a small Spanish onion in the water with the ham. When the ham is tender leave it in the water until it is nearly cold to keep the flesh moist and improve the flavour.

JELLY—To set quickly: Stand the mould in a basin. Fill the basin with water reaching nearly to the top of the mould, then put a handful of kitchen salt in the water. The jelly will set in half the usual time.

LETTUCE—To crisp: A few drops of lemon juice added to the rinsing water will make the lettuce crisp.

MILK—To prevent boiling over: Place a wooden spoon in the saucepan of milk just before it comes to the boil and the milk will not boil over.

OMELETTE—Always let the butter be smoking hot before adding your mixture to the pan. This avoids sticking.

PARSLEY—To dry for storage: Take a bunch of parsley, and holding it by the stems, dip it in boiling water until it is a vivid green. Put it in a quick oven to dry. Rub between your hands or through a coarse sieve.

PEELING ONIONS—Begin at the root end and peel upwards, then the odour will scarcely effect your eyes at all.

PEPPER POTS—To prevent clogs: Place a dried pea in the pot and it will prevent the holes in the lid from becoming clogged.

POTATOES—To bake: Potatoes will bake more quickly if they are first allowed to stand in hot water for 15 minutes.

POTATOES, MASHED—A sprinkle of baking powder added to potatoes while mashing makes them much lighter.

POULTRY—To keep fresh: Place a large peeled onion inside the birds that are not to be used or cooked for a day or two.

RICE—To boil: Add a little lemon juice to the water. This makes the rice white and grainy when cooked.

SALT CELLAR—To prevent clogging: Place a few grains of rice in the salt cellar. This will absorb any dampness and prevent clogging.

GUIDE TO OVEN SETTINGS

	GAS	ELEC °F	ELEC °C
VERY SLOW	$\frac{1}{4}-\frac{1}{2}$	225	110
SLOW	1	275	140
SLOW	2	300	150
MODERATE	3	325	160
MODERATE	4	350	180
FAIRLY HOT	5	375	190
FAIRLY HOT	6	400	200
HOT	7	425	220
VERY HOT	8	450	230
VERY HOT	9	475	240

INDEX

136

NOTES

NOTES

NOTES

NOTES

NOTES

NOTES